2022

NFL Draft Preview

The Athletic

TRIUMPH
BOOKS

Library of Congress Cataloging-in-Publication Data available upon
request.

This book is available in quantity at special discounts for your group
or organization. For further information, contact:

Triumph Books LLC
814 North Franklin Street
Chicago, Illinois 60610
(312) 337-0747
www.triumphbooks.com

Printed in U.S.A.
ISBN: 978-1-63727-138-4

Design by Patricia Frey

All photos courtesy of AP Images

Contents

6   **Introduction**
BY DANE BRUGLER

11   **Top 100 NFL Draft Board**
BY DANE BRUGLER

39   **Two-round Mock Draft**
BY DANE BRUGLER

55   **Positional Rankings**
BY DANE BRUGLER

131   **Player Profiles**
IKEM EKWONU • SAUCE GARDNER • MALIK WILLIS
KENNY PICKETT • DRAKE LONDON

169   **The Freaks List**
BY BRUCE FELDMAN

191   **Calendar of Events**

NFL Draft
2022

There is talent in the 2022 NFL Draft, but teams will have to look for it

by Dane Brugler

Roger Staubach once told me that he didn't know he was drafted until he read it in the newspaper the next day.

To say times have changed would be an understatement.

Today, the NFL Draft does better television ratings than the NBA finals and the Academy Awards. The event is a traveling road show year-to-year from Nashville to Cleveland and soon to be Las Vegas for the 2022 NFL Draft on April 28-30.

As the game of football continues to grow in popularity, so does the draft. Why? Because it represents hope, for both fans and front offices. Some of the NFL's best players were top-10 picks (Patrick Mahomes, Josh Allen, Nick Bosa), but most weren't (Aaron Rodgers, TJ Watt, Aaron Donald). Some weren't even drafted in the first round (Travis Kelce, Davante Adams, Deebo Samuel).

Every NFL Draft produces Pro Bowlers, and this year's class won't be any different — it's up to NFL teams to find them. However, the identity of this year's draft is a little different than most. The best way to sum up the 2022 draft class: A lackluster group at the top and a conundrum of quarterbacks, but intriguing depth in the early-to-mid rounds at almost every other position.

The 2022 NFL Draft might lack star power at the top — there is no Myles Garrett, Joe Burrow, or a no-brainer No. 1 overall pick like most years. In fact, it would be a stretch to use the word "elite" for any of the prospects in this draft. However, the overall depth of this class is what has NFL evaluators excited.

Arguably the most important position in football aside from quarterback, pass rusher is the unquestioned strength of this year's draft class. Michigan's Aidan Hutchinson and Oregon's Kayvon Thibodeaux should be two of the first players drafted, maybe as early as the first two picks. Hutchinson doesn't have the same bend or arc skills as the Bosa brothers, but he wins with similar quickness, power and skilled hand play. Thibodeaux might not be on Chase Young's level as a pass rusher, but he understands how to create leverage as a pass rusher with his length, flexibility, and agility.

The run on first-round pass rushers should continue with Georgia's Travon Walker, Purdue's George Karlaftis, Michigan's David Ojabo, Florida State's Jermaine Johnson and possibly a few other names like Penn State's Arnold Ebiketie or Houston's Logan Hall. And then on day two, there are several intriguing names like Miami (Ohio)'s Dominique Robinson or Cincinnati's Myjai Sanders.

A new collection of talented pass rushers entering the league is bad news for teams with pass protection issues. But the good news is that this year's offensive line group boasts a host of future NFL starters and mirrors the pass rushers in ways. At the top, there are a few offensive tackles with a legitimate chance at being the No. 1 pick.

Alabama's Evan Neal has a rare mix of size, athleticism and flexibility. NC State's Ikem Ekwonu is nimble, powerful, and should continue to get better as his technique and awareness catch up to his explosive physical traits. Mississippi State's Charles Cross lacks ideal power, but he processes things quickly and shows outstanding hand exchange and movement patterns in pass protection.

Northern Iowa's Trevor Penning, Central Michigan's Bernard Raimann and Minnesota's Daniel Faalele are three more blockers with a chance at the first round, followed by several other day two offensive tackles with starting potential.

Wide receiver will be well represented in the first-round with a variety of different ice cream flavors. If you want size and above-the-rim ability, USC's Drake London is the target. If a team is looking for this year's Deebo Samuel, albeit in a bigger body, then Arkansas' Treylon Burks will be an attractive option. Every team needs a player who can get open before and after the catch, which is why Ohio State's Garrett Wilson is favored to be the first pass-catcher off the board.

There isn't a slam-dunk first rounder among the running backs and tight ends, but both positions will be well represented on days two and three. We might see a linebacker (Utah's Devin Lloyd) and safety (Notre Dame's Kyle Hamilton) drafted in the top-10, but the sweet spot for both positions will be on day two.

There are several other positions worth discussing, but I've put it off long enough — let's talk quarterbacks.

Beauty is in the eye of the beholder, and that is never more true than this draft class of quarterbacks.

It is hard to look at this class and say with conviction that there is a quarterback who, at some point in their careers, will lead a team to the playoffs and establish himself as a top-15 quarterback in the NFL. But there are several intriguing options, starting with Pittsburgh's Kenny Pickett, who took a massive jump in his consistency and production as a senior. Though he doesn't have an explosive arm and must improve his pocket presence, Pickett is accurate at all three levels and has the mobility to move the pocket.

Pickett is probably the favorite to be the first quarterback drafted, but Ole Miss' Matt Corral and Liberty's Malik Willis have higher ceilings. Corral is like a point guard in basketball or shortstop in baseball — everything he does is quick-twitch, and he competes with the athletic instincts to create plays. Willis is an electric athlete and delivers the ball with velocity, although both he and Corral must improve the consistency of their decisions within the structure of the offense. North Carolina's Sam Howell, who will draw Baker Mayfield comparisons, is well-liked around the league. Cincinnati's Desmond Ridder put together a 43-6 record as the Bearcats' starter, including a trip to the College Football Playoff. Nevada's Carson Strong needs to be cleared medically, but NFL coaches will be drawn to his arm talent.

Despite the question marks, quarterback desperation is a real thing in the NFL. And with few general managers and head coaches promised "next year," teams will roll the dice on these talented, yet flawed passers as early as the first-round.

Time will tell how each draft pick plays out, but at least for now, they represent what each fan base covets: hope.

—Dane Brugler

Top 100 NFL Draft Board for 2022

No. 1 Aidan Hutchinson
first of five edge rushers
in Dane Brugler's top 15

Draft Board

The initial steps of the postseason draft process are now in the rear view mirror.

The underclassmen deadline came and went with 100 draft-eligible players officially declaring for the 2022 NFL Draft. The all-star circuit was helpful as hundreds of players had the opportunity to audition for teams at the Senior Bowl, East-West Shrine Bowl, NFLPA Collegiate Bowl and other events.

Next comes the Scouting Combine, pro day workouts and team visits.

There are no changes among the top five, with Michigan's Aidan Hutchinson leading the way at No. 1 followed by NC State's Ikem Ekwonu, Alabama's Evan Neal, Oregon's Kayvon Thibodeaux and Notre Dame's Kyle Hamilton. The all-star circuit gave a positive boost to several prospects (Hello, Travis Jones), and there will be some more fluctuation after the combine and workouts.

1
Aidan Hutchinson
Edge, Michigan (6-6, 261)

It's understandable why some might balk at the thought of Hutchinson going No. 1. He's not Myles Garrett or Chase Young and probably wouldn't have been a top-10 pick in last year's draft. But that is the reality of this draft class. Although he doesn't have the same bend or arc skills as the Bosa brothers, Hutchinson wins with similar quickness, power and skilled hand play to be productive as both a pass rusher and run defender. His arms are going to measure much shorter than many would expect, but he is scheme-proof and should be a consistent double-digit sack producer over his career.

2 Ikem Ekwonu
OT, NC State (6-4, 322)

I received mixed reactions (from both fans and evaluators around the league) to my mock draft 2.0 that had Ekwonu at No. 1 overall. Some believe the Jaguars go pass rusher or Alabama's Evan Neal, but several others agreed with the possibility of "Ickey" at No. 1 because he is one of the best players in the draft. Although his game needs refinement, especially with his over-setting, Ekwonu is nimble, powerful and should only continue to get better as his technique and awareness mature.

3 Evan Neal
OT, Alabama (6-7, 357)

A smooth athlete for a massive blocker, Neal bends well in pass protection and continues to rework his feet into position, using controlled hand exchange to keep rushers contained. In the run game, he has strong hands and does well at initial contact as a drive blocker, but his balance and sustain skills start to fade as the play progresses. Neal lacks elite lateral agility and needs to clean up his leaning, but he is an effective blocker due to his rare mix of size, athleticism and flexibility, also offering legitimate position versatility.

4 Kayvon Thibodeaux
Edge, Oregon (6-4, 255)

Talking with evaluators around the league, the feedback on Thibodeaux is a lot of "He's really talented, but ..." reactions. He is not universally loved — for a variety of reasons — but most still believe he fits somewhere into the top seven picks. Although not on the same level as past pass rushers who were drafted this early, Thibodeaux understands how to create leverage as a pass rusher with his length, flexibility and agility.

5 Kyle Hamilton
DS, Notre Dame (6-3, 218)

A long, supersized safety, Hamilton has the explosive range, smarts and toughness to be deployed anywhere on the football field. He anticipates well vs. both the pass and the run and shows the ball skills and tackling balance to be a consistent finisher. Hopefully he lands in a defensive scheme that understands how to best maximize his talent because Hamilton can be a diverse matchup weapon thanks to to his rare skill set.

6 Travon Walker
Edge, Georgia (6-5, 275)

I know I'm higher on Walker than most, but I'm okay with that — I'm betting on his rare traits. He has impressive movement skills for a 275-pounder, including an explosive first step to shoot through gaps, cross the face of blockers or chase down plays. He wasn't asked to be a consistent outside rusher in the Bulldogs' scheme, but that helped him develop into a strong run defender, disengaging and leveraging blocks. Walker is still developing his sequencing plan as a pass rusher, but he has freaky athletic traits for his size and offers the natural power and length to consistently win his matchups. He projects as a scheme-diverse end with the ceiling to be one of the best NFL defenders from this draft class.

7 Devin Lloyd
LB, Utah (6-3, 232)

A do-everything, four-down linebacker, Lloyd plays with speed and suddenness in his movements to weave through traffic in pursuit or change directions and make plays in coverage. He has room to improve his play strength and posture as a take-on player, but he does a great job scraping and sifting with his slippery athleticism and length to make plays at the line of scrimmage. Lloyd is a better version of the Chargers' Kenneth Murray when he was coming out of Oklahoma.

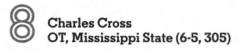 Charles Cross
OT, Mississippi State (6-5, 305)

Opinions are split on Cross around the league. Some believe he belongs in the top half of round one, but others see another Andre Dillard and aren't completely sold. He doesn't have ideal power, but Cross is outstanding in pass protection, and that is the basis for his high grade. He processes things quickly and shows outstanding hand exchange and movement patterns to frustrate pass rushers. With Cross, I see a future starter with Pro Bowl potential.

Derek Stingley Jr.
CB, LSU (6-1, 195)

The ultimate enigma in the 2022 draft class. If you swapped Stingley's 2019 and 2021 seasons, he would probably be the unquestioned first pick in this draft. But he is a tough player to figure out because the past two seasons weren't anything like his All-American freshman year. The main issue has been health, but is that something teams should expect to follow him to the NFL? The combine (medicals and interviews) will be a monumental step for Stingley as teams prepare to put a final grade on him.

10 Ahmad Gardner
CB, Cincinnati (6-2, 190)

Another prospect with mixed feedback from NFL teams, Gardner put together an impressive three-year career for the Bearcats with nine interceptions and zero touchdowns allowed on his watch. You have to hunt for targets on his 2021 film because he was rarely challenged. He needs to improve his poise downfield, but he is a sticky bump-and-run corner with the athletic instincts to make plays. Cincinnati hasn't produced a first round pick since 1971, but that should change soon.

Derek Stingley Jr. – No. 9

11 Garrett Wilson
WR, Ohio State (6-0, 186)

With his ability to get open before and after the catch, Wilson is the type of receiver that makes the playbook come alive. Despite his average size, he makes unbelievable adjustments on the football and is comfortable with bodies around him. With his slender frame, elite body control and catch point skills, Wilson reminds me of CeeDee Lamb.

12 Trent McDuffie
CB, Washington (5-11, 195)

McDuffie shut down opposing receivers on his 2021 tape and is very well-liked among NFL scouts. There are a few things working against him — he has ordinary size and ball production (10 passes defended and two interceptions in 28 games played). But McDuffie is a composed, springy athlete (will jump somewhere in the low 40-inches in the vertical) with the cover awareness to be a long-time NFL cover man.

13 Treylon Burks
WR, Arkansas (6-3, 232)

With his vision and acceleration, Burks has the skills to turn quick-hitters into big plays, breaking tackles with his balance, body strength and competitive toughness (led the SEC with 22 plays of 20-plus yards in 2021). He can also track the football downfield with his large catch radius, although his separation skills are mitigated by his undeveloped rhythm as a route runner. As long as he stays healthy, Burks has the skills to grow into an NFL team's No. 1 receiver with some similarities to a linebacker-sized version of Deebo Samuel.

14 David Ojabo
Edge, Michigan (6-5, 255)

An athletic rusher with a long, nimble frame, Ojabo has the balanced feet and hip flexibility developed from years of basketball and soccer training to work tight spaces and grease the edge as a pass rusher. His defensive role shouldn't be restricted to only rushing the passer, but he needs to improve his functional strength and body positioning to make plays in the run game. Ojabo is admittedly "still learning" various aspects of football, but he is naturally explosive with the upfield burst and stride length to overwhelm tackles with arc speed. He projects as a subpackage rusher as a rookie with Pro Bowl potential down the road.

15 Jermaine Johnson
Edge, Florida State (6-4, 259)

Johnson went to Mobile as the top defensive player on the roster and left the same way, dominating throughout the week. The Georgia transfer bet on himself and became the alpha of the Seminoles' defensive line in 2021, leading the ACC in tackles for loss (18.0) and sacks (12.0). Johnson has the length, agility and active hands that lead to disruption as both a pass rusher and run defender and projects as an every-down NFL starter.

16 Drake London
WR, USC (6-5, 212)

The ultimate respect for a wide receiver is when everyone knows the ball is going to him yet the defense can't stop it, and that sums up London's junior season (averaged 15 targets per game). That season also was his first in his life as a football-only athlete. His basketball background is evident with his elite highpointing skills to play through contact and thrive above the rim.

17 Tyler Linderbaum
OC, Iowa (6-3, 292)

A six-sport athlete in high school, Linderbaum is very quick in his snap-and-step and shows athletic range, body control and refinement as an on-the-move or reach blocker. Although he doesn't have an ideal body type, his wrestling background is clear with his handwork, leverage and killer instinct to win early or reset mid-rep. Overall, Linderbaum lacks ideal arm length and will struggle at times in pass protection, but he is an elite-level run blocker because of his athleticism and grip strength to latch-and-drive.

18 Andrew Booth Jr.
CB, Clemson (6-0, 193)

There is volatility to Booth's game, which comes with the territory of playing cornerback with an aggressive mindset. He has room to improve his feel for spacing, but Booth plays with three important ingredients to playing the position at a high level: fluid athleticism, the ability to find the football and catch point disruption skills. Plug him into a man-heavy scheme and let him continue to grow.

19 Trevor Penning
OT, Northern Iowa (6-7, 330)

Coming from the FCS level, Penning is still raw in several areas, which was clear during Senior Bowl practices. But tackles with his combination of size, length (almost 35-inch arms), power and athleticism are uncommon. Penning also loves to play pissed off, and his compete skills will translate well to the pro game.

Tyler Linderbaum – No. 17

20 Nakobe Dean
LB, Georgia (6-0, 225)

After winning the 2018 Butkus Award in high school as the nation's top linebacker, Dean did the same three years later at Georgia as the 2021 Butkus Award winner. The soul of the Bulldogs' national championship-winning defense, he doesn't have ideal size, but his key/read/flow skills and play range are both outstanding. In a lot of ways, Dean projects as Jonathan Vilma 2.0.

21 George Karlaftis
Edge, Purdue (6-4, 268)

Born and raised in Athens, Greece, Karlaftis moved to the United States and adopted football as his go-to sport, finishing his college career with 30.5 tackles for loss over 27 games. His hands are not only physical and violent, but they're well timed and strategic to get the offense off schedule. You wish his arms were longer and he had more twitch in his movements, but Karlaftis has NFL power, effort and hand work to break down the rhythm of blockers.

22 Jameson Williams
WR, Alabama (6-2, 182)

If not for his recent ACL injury, Williams would be about 10 spots higher on this list. Born into a track family, he has elite speed in his routes and with the ball in his hands. And he is more than just speed, tracking the ball well downfield and making easy adjustments on the football. In a downfield passing offense in the NFL, Williams has a chance to be special — as long as his knee makes a full recovery.

23 Daxton Hill
DS, Michigan (6-0, 192)

Arguably the top nickel defender in the draft, Hill can cover wide receivers and tight ends while also providing a thump in the run game and as a blitzer. Although he has the size of a cornerback, he should test off the charts and plays with the toughness of a safety. With his versatile skills, Hill is exactly what several teams are searching for in their secondaries.

24 Kenyon Green
OG, Texas A&M (6-4, 325)

After starting at right guard as a freshman and left guard as a sophomore, Green was the only returning starter on the Aggies' offensive line as a junior and was asked to fill in across the line, becoming the only NCAA player with 80-plus snaps at four different offensive line positions in 2021. He must fix the bad habits and penalties at the next level, but Green does a great job staying balanced before and after contact with the mobility and brawling mentality to win his matchups.

25 Chris Olave
WR, Ohio State (6-1, 182)

The Buckeyes' all-time leader in touchdown catches (35), Olave is a smooth route runner with the deep speed and tracking instincts to consistent win down the field. He has an average body type and doesn't consistently create after the catch, but he knows how to create spacing and shows a feel for leveraging coverage. Olave is a polished pass catcher with NFL-ready skills.

26   Zion Johnson
OG, Boston College (6-3, 314)

Johnson has a stout, developed body type with the patience and placement to plant and re-leverage himself to stay centered as a pass blocker. In the run game, he shows off his body control and drive strength to execute from various angles. Overall, Johnson will occasionally lose his balance, but his combination of play strength, muscle twitch and reaction skills help him sustain consistently. He has the talent to carve out a decade-long career as an interior NFL blocker.

27   Devonte Wyatt
DT, Georgia (6-3, 307)

With his athletic traits, Wyatt can win in different ways off the ball, displaying initial quickness, lateral range and chase down speed. In the run game, he understands how to leverage gaps and find the ball carrier, although I want to see him become a better finisher. Overall, Wyatt needs to play with better control, but he fires off the ball and competes with the speed and effort to make an impact on all three downs.

28   Jordan Davis
DT, Georgia (6-6, 360)

Despite high pad level, Davis is a hard-to-move space eater with the point-of-attack strength to reestablish the line of scrimmage and overwhelm ball carriers as a tackler. He is a talented athlete for a player his size, and his motor expands his tackling range, but he was also helped by fewer defensive snaps in 2021 (25.2 per game) compared to 2020 (32.9). I'm not super high on Davis like others because he is limited as a pass rusher, but he has the size, functional power and block recognition to be a dominant run defender.

29
Bernhard Raimann
OT, Central Michigan (6-6, 304)

An Austrian native, Raimann has one of the most unlikely journeys of any prospect in this draft class. He made the transition from tight end to left tackle during the pandemic and blossomed into a first-round caliber player due to his athletic reflexes, natural balance and stubborn hands. Despite only 18 career games on the offensive line in his life, Raimann should compete for starting reps during his NFL rookie season.

30
Jahan Dotson
WR, Penn State (5-11, 175)

Dotson puts defenders in conflict with his twitchy speed to defeat press and manipulate coverages at the stem. Although he is undersized, he has above-average hands and natural body control with maybe the largest catch radius of any sub 5-foot-11 receiver I have ever scouted. Dotson isn't a tackle-breaker, and his marginal play strength will be more noticeable vs. NFL defenders, but his dynamic speed, route instincts and ball skills make him a difficult player to cover one-on-one.

31
Kenny Pickett
QB, Pittsburgh (6-3, 217)

Pickett shows outstanding instincts as a passer with his ability to throw receivers open, keep his eyes on schedule and make quick-reaction decisions. Though his confidence is more of a strength than weakness, he will get greedy at times, forcing throws into tight coverage and writing checks his arm can't cash. Overall, Pickett has some skittish tendencies, and the hand size (throws with a glove) will be a factor for some teams, but his football IQ, functional mobility and accuracy from various platforms are a special package.

32 Malik Willis
QB, Liberty (6-0, 220)

Although his timing and accuracy go through lulls, Willis has a fluid release, outstanding velocity and a great feel for touch and placement on vertical-based patterns. With his escapability and body strength, the backfield was his playground, but he struggles to recognize pressures and takes too many sacks (No. 1 in the FBS with 51 sacks in 2021). Overall, Willis requires time to mature his anticipation, vision and accuracy, but he has the potential to be a dynamic NFL playmaker due to his natural athleticism, arm talent and intangibles.

33 Logan Hall
Edge, Houston (6-6, 278)

Although he played primarily inside in college, Hall has the long levers and foot quickness to be an impactful pass rusher when given a runway off the edge. He has the body flexibility to bend, dip and attack from different angles but must continue to develop his anchor and shed strength, especially when his pad level rises. Hall has some tweener traits and lacks consistency, but with additional coaching, he can be a matchup weapon because of his athletic versatility, body length, and disruptive nature.

34 Arnold Ebiketie
Edge, Penn State (6-2, 250)

A Temple transfer, Ebiketie explodes off the edge and stresses blockers with his arc acceleration, active hands and relentless play personality (registered at least one tackle for loss in 11 of 12 games in 2021). Though he uses his length well as a pass rusher, he struggles to consistently anchor, lock out and free himself to contain the run. Ebiketie needs to improve his refinement as a rusher and reliability vs. the run, but he is a long, twitched-up athlete with the motor and mentality to develop into a starting NFL pass rusher.

35 Matt Corral
QB, Ole Miss (6-2, 205)

Like a shortstop in baseball or point guard in basketball, Corral is quick in everything he does — from his feet to his eyes to his release. He played in a quarterback-friendly offense and faces a learning curve in the NFL, but he has the athleticism and passing twitch to be a playmaker. When discussing Corral, every scout has mentioned the interview process as the most important step for his draft grade.

36 Jalen Pitre
DS, Baylor (5-11, 196)

Playing the hybrid "Star" position in Dave Aranda's scheme, Pitre is an exercise of "Where's Waldo" on tape. From play-to-play, he moved from edge rusher to slot corner to traditional safety, which allowed him to show off his toughness in the run game (18.0 tackles for loss in 2021) and coverage skills. Along with his strong week in Mobile, Pitre is a player trending up.

37 Sam Howell
QB, North Carolina (6-0, 221)

The Howell-to-Baker Mayfield comparisons are going to overused, but with good reason — they make sense. They have similar size, builds and arms, although Howell has more juice as a scrambler. The North Carolina passer didn't have the 2021 season many expected, but he has all the requisite traits to start games in the NFL.

38 Kingsley Enagbare
Edge, South Carolina (6-4, 261)

Enagbare rushes with heavy, skilled hands and forward lean to convert his speed to power and does a nice job with his rush sequencing to set traps for blockers. He is rugged and alert but will need to become more consistent setting the edge in the run game and proving he can kick inside on passing downs. Although he has tightness in his movements and lacks suddenness, Enagbare is efficient and powerful in his attack with the athletic movements to break down blockers.

39 Kaiir Elam
CB, Florida (6-2, 200)

Elam checks boxes for size, strength, physicality and athleticism, mixing it up with receivers and crowding the catch point downfield. He will surrender spacing on stop and comeback routes, which can be masked by coaching and scheme, but slight stiffness in his mirror and transitions will always be there. With his physicality for press-man, he reminds me of Tampa Bay's Carlton Davis when Davis was coming out of Auburn.

40 Kenneth Walker III
RB, Michigan State (5-10, 212)

There is no consensus RB1 in this draft class, but if there is a running back who might be considered in the first round, it should be Walker. With his vision and contact balance, he generates impressive burst off his plant foot to dart away from trouble and break tackles (led the FBS with 89 forced missed tackles in 2021). He must improve as a pass catcher and pass protector, but his instinctive ability to set up his cuts and create yardage will translate to the pro game.

41 Desmond Ridder
QB, Cincinnati (6-3, 207)

A tall, lean passer, Ridder moves with light feet and is comfortable making throws on the move. His release gets a tad long and his accuracy needs to be more consistent, but Ridder has enjoyed a lot of success on the football field because of his confidence and willingness to use the entire field. He will compete for starting reps early in his career.

42 Darian Kinnard
OG, Kentucky (6-5, 324)

Kinnard looks to impose his will early and manhandle everything in his path to create movement at the point of attack. He has the quickness to square half-man rushers, but he relies more on his upper body than lower body to get the job done, which leads to balance issues. Overall, Kinnard's NFL ceiling will hinge on his ability to refine his sloppy tendencies, but he has the physical tools and bully mentality to be a dominant, scheme-diverse run blocker, either at tackle or guard.

43 Roger McCreary
CB, Auburn (5-11, 189)

Once the third-lowest-ranked recruit in Auburn's 2018 class, McCreary worked his way up the depth chart and proved himself as one of the best defensive players in the SEC the past two seasons. He will be eliminated from several draft boards because his short arms (29 1/4 inches), but he plays sticky with the awareness and willingness to mix things up with receivers. McCreary has inside/outside versatility and should compete for a starting role early in his NFL career.

44 Quay Walker
LB, Georgia (6-4, 245)

Although he doesn't have the résumé of a playmaker as a one-year starter, Walker aces the eye test with his combination of size, length and athleticism. He has outstanding mirroring skills vs. the run and uses his long arms to punch himself off blocks or lasso ball carriers out of his reach. With his traits and budding instincts, Walker's best football should be ahead of him.

45 Travis Jones
DT, Connecticut (6-4, 326)

A big-bodied athlete with strong legs and arms, Jones is quick off the ball and powerful through his hips to be disruptive vs. both the pass and the run. He uses quickness and forceful hand moves to get his nose in the gap, but he needs to harness his momentum and consistently use his secondary moves to shoot through. Overall, Jones' pass rush technique is still a work in progress, but he creates problems for interior blockers with his athletic movements and explosive upper body to stack, shed and toss.

46 Chad Muma
LB, Wyoming (6-2, 241)

Averaging 11.3 tackles per game over the past two seasons, Muma's college film is catnip for NFL teams. He can run, fill up the stat sheet and boasts top-notch intangibles. I want to see him be more physical as a take-on player, but he is a high-energy tackling machine with the play speed and awareness to always be around the football.

47 Jalen Tolbert
WR, South Alabama (6-1, 195)

After bypassing scholarship offers from Power 5 programs to stay close to home, Tolbert became the most prolific receiver in South Alabama history, including the first player in school history to reach 1,000 receiving yards in a season (and he did it twice). Although he doesn't have elite top-end speed, Tolbert has fluid footwork and uses slight hesitation in his route breaks so he can mash the gas and create pockets of separation.

48 Christian Harris
LB, Alabama (6-2, 232)

Harris is a do-everything breed of linebacker with the multi-dimensional skill set to drop in coverage, get downhill vs. the run or make plays in the backfield as a blitzer. He has a good feel for play direction but needs to pull the trigger a half-second quicker and better leverage his gaps as a take-on player. Overall, Harris must become more consistent diagnosing the action, but he is a versatile athlete with the play speed and intangibles to grow into a dependable NFL starter.

49 Jamaree Salyer
OG, Georgia (6-3, 320)

A college left tackle who is ideally suited inside at guard, Salyer is very efficient in his set-up and plays with outstanding body control, balance and core strength to stay centered through contact. Although he tends to get narrow with his steps and has some bad habits, he understands depth, angles and how to effectively respond with his hands. He projects as a plug-and-play NFL guard while offering position versatility in a pinch.

50 John Metchie III
WR, Alabama (5-11, 196)

Metchie, who lived on three different continents before his seventh birthday, adopted a fierce work ethic and devotion to his craft, which is evident on film. He has only average size and speed but is an instinctive route runner who understands how to manipulate coverage and be a quarterback's best friend. As long as he makes a full recovery from his ACL tear, he should be a quality No. 2 receiver in the NFL.

Prospects 51-100

RANK	NAME	POS.	SCHOOL	HT, WT
51	DeMarvin Leal	DT	Texas A&M	6-4, 290
52	Daniel Faalele	OT	Minnesota	6-8, 387
53	Perrion Winfrey	DT	Oklahoma	6-4, 303
54	Drake Jackson	Edge	USC	6-4, 255
55	Isaiah Spiller	RB	Texas A&M	6-1, 215
56	Lewis Cine	DS	Georgia	6-1, 200
57	Phidarian Mathis	DT	Alabama	6-4, 313
58	Myjai Sanders	Edge	Cincinnati	6-4, 242
59	Breece Hall	RB	Iowa State	6-1, 220
60	Trey McBride	TE	Colorado State	6-3, 249
61	Leo Chenal	LB	Wisconsin	6-2, 252
62	Jaquan Brisker	DS	Penn State	6-1, 203
63	Jeremy Ruckert	TE	Ohio State	6-5, 250
64	Max Mitchell	OT	Louisiana	6-6, 299
65	Brian Asamoah	LB	Oklahoma	6-0, 222
66	Alex Wright	Edge	UAB	6-7, 270
67	George Pickens	WR	Georgia	6-3, 203
68	Kyler Gordon	CB	Washington	6-0, 195
69	David Bell	WR	Purdue	6-2, 207
70	Dylan Parham	OC	Memphis	6-2, 313
71	Isaiah Likely	TE	Coastal Carolina	6-4, 241
72	Marcus Jones	CB	Houston	5-9, 185
73	Tariq Woolen	CB	UTSA	6-3, 205
74	Channing Tindall	LB	Georgia	6-2, 223
75	Boye Mafe	Edge	Minnesota	6-4, 255
76	Troy Andersen	LB	Montana State	6-4, 235
77	Wan'Dale Robinson	WR	Kentucky	5-10, 187
78	Greg Dulcich	TE	UCLA	6-4, 248
79	Skyy Moore	WR	Western Michigan	5-9, 195
80	Ed Ingram	OG	LSU	6-3, 317
81	Marquis Hayes	OG	Oklahoma	6-5, 330
82	Dominique Robinson	Edge	Miami (Ohio)	6-5, 254
83	Abraham Lucas	OT	Washington State	6-2, 322

RANK	NAME	POS.	SCHOOL	HT, WT
84	DeAngelo Malone	Edge	Western Kentucky	6-3, 234
85	Tyler Smith	OT	Tulsa	6-5, 332
86	Bryan Cook	DS	Cincinnati	6-1, 205
87	Martin Emerson	CB	Mississippi State	6-1, 202
88	Cameron Thomas	Edge	San Diego State	6-4, 264
89	Nicholas Petit-Frere	OT	Ohio State	6-5, 304
90	Justyn Ross	WR	Clemson	6-4, 209
91	Tyler Allgeier	RB	BYU	5-11, 221
92	Jesse Luketa	Edge	Penn State	6-2, 261
93	Kyren Williams	RB	Notre Dame	5-9, 199
94	Coby Bryant	CB	Cincinnati	6-1, 191
95	Kerby Joseph	DS	Illinois	6-1, 200
96	Christian Watson	WR	North Dakota State	6-4, 211
97	Lecitus Smith	OG	Virginia Tech	6-3, 321
98	John Ridgeway	DT	Arkansas	6-5, 327
99	Damone Clark	LB	LSU	6-2, 240
100	Carson Strong	QB	Nevada	6-4, 226

Two-round 2022 NFL Mock Draft

Dane Brugler's mock 2.0 has a new No. 1 pick and more surprises

First Round

In most NFL Drafts, there are five to seven top-tier prospects who make up the "upper class" and will be the first players drafted. That is followed by 12-15 "middle class" players who might not be elite but received first-round grades from teams and project as solid NFL starters.

The bad news is the 2022 NFL Draft is missing those "upper class" prospects — there is no Joe Burrow or Myles Garrett or Ja'Marr Chase this year.

The good news is this year's draft is well-stocked with "middle class" first-rounders — players with NFL starting traits who will make impacts as rookies.

Not having those top-tier players in this class will make the first-round, especially the top 10, even more unpredictable than usual. There are surprises every year, but we should expect them early in the 2022 NFL Draft as draft boards from team to team might look wildly different.

1 Jacksonville Jaguars
Ikem Ekwonu, OT, NC State

After numerous conversations with NFL scouts and league execs in preparation for this mock, there were two key takeaways that led me to Ekwonu here. First, there are several evaluators around the league who have Ekwonu ranked higher than Alabama's Evan Neal and Mississippi State's Charles Cross. Second, several evaluators agreed that in a draft class missing a no-brainer top prospect, they prefer the tackles over the pass rushers. I have no clue how the Jaguars feel, but Ekwonu at least belongs in this conversation.

A three-year starter at NC State, Ekwonu has impressive movements for his size and generates extraordinary explosion at contact. He lacks refinement and is guilty of over-setting, but he is nimble, powerful and should get better and better as his technique and awareness mature. Ekwonu's tape shows a tackle who can also play guard, not the other way around.

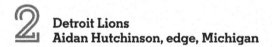

2 Detroit Lions
Aidan Hutchinson, edge, Michigan

A Week 18 victory against the Packers meant the Lions lost the No. 1 overall pick, but there is a decent chance that the top-ranked player on Detroit's draft board will still be available at No. 2.

Hutchinson isn't on the same level as the Bosa brothers — he doesn't have the same bend or arc skills. However, there are similarities when you talk about their quickness, power and skilled hand play to defeat blockers and disrupt the pocket. Hutchinson can win in multiple ways and is wired in a way that will appeal to head coach Dan Campbell.

3 Houston Texans
Kayvon Thibodeaux, edge, Oregon

Is there a quarterback in this draft class who is a clear upgrade over Davis Mills? I don't think so, and I doubt the Texans will either. Thibodeaux isn't universally loved around the league, but he is one of the more talented players in this draft. He knows how to create leverage as a pass rusher due to his length and athleticism and is highly physical vs. the run.

Fans expecting Myles Garrett or Chase Young will be disappointed, but that doesn't mean Thibodeaux can't make an immediate impact of his own.

4 New York Jets
Derek Stingley Jr., CB, LSU

The Jets could go in a number of different directions here. Alabama's Evan Neal could start at right guard as a rookie and be the long-term answer at right tackle (and provide Mekhi Becton insurance at left tackle). But Stingley would give the Jets a cover man with the talent to be a legitimate No. 1 cornerback, something the franchise has missed since Darrelle Revis.

Stingley set the bar high after his All-American freshman season as part of LSU's national championship team. And although the last two seasons haven't gone according to plan, the talent is still there. Stingley's draft stock is extremely volatile right now, and his interviews and medicals will ultimately determine whether he is drafted this high or falls out of the top 10.

5 New York Giants
Evan Neal, OT, Alabama

Slowly but surely, Andrew Thomas is progressing at left tackle, but the right tackle spot was a glaring weak spot for the Giants this past season. Nate Solder has likely played his last snap with the franchise, and Matt Peart hasn't done enough to keep the Giants from finding an upgrade this offseason.

Neal has functional experience at guard and both tackle spots and would be an immediate improvement on the Giants' offensive line depth chart. His balance will fade as the play progresses, but he has a rare mix of size, athleticism and flexibility to make plays in pass protection and the run game.

Carolina Panthers
Charles Cross, OT, Mississippi State

If the Panthers strike out on their quarterback options in free agency and on the trade market, this could be the spot where we see the first quarterback drafted. This is Carolina's only draft pick in the top 100, putting even more pressure on Matt Rhule and the organization to get this selection right.

Cross is talented enough to be OT1 on some team's draft boards. He has the athleticism and movement patterns to be comfortable pass-blocking on an island, and his hands are well-timed and precise. Cross should be able to start from day one as a rookie.

New York Giants (from Chicago)
Kyle Hamilton, DS, Notre Dame

Safety isn't the most glaring need on the Giants' depth chart, but with a new general manager and head coach, they will be looking to draft impact players, above everything else, in the top 10. And Hamilton might be the most talented player in the draft, regardless of position.

At 6-3 and 218 pounds, Hamilton is a super-sized safety with the range and length to be a matchup weapon in the NFL. Though his physical traits stand out, it is his football IQ that is most impressive, sensing what is about to happen and being disruptive.

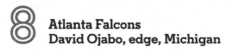

8 Atlanta Falcons
David Ojabo, edge, Michigan

Predictably, the Falcons finished dead-last in the NFL in sacks this season as they sorely lack the edge rush talent to keep offenses off-balance. Still young in football years, Ojabo is still a work in progress, but he has the talent level right now to stress blockers.

Polling several NFL personnel people for this mock, the feedback on Ojabo was he won't be a top-10 pick because of his struggles vs. the run and his relative inexperience. But I'm betting on his ceiling at a premium position to bump him up in this draft class.

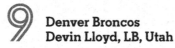

9 Denver Broncos
Devin Lloyd, LB, Utah

The Broncos said "no thanks" to Justin Fields and Mac Jones at No. 9 overall last year. Will they pass on the quarterback position again a year later? We'll see if Denver is able to find an upgrade at the position prior to the draft or if it buys into one of the quarterbacks in this draft class.

Denver landed an impact defender with the ninth pick last year, and it could do that again with Lloyd. A former safety, he has outstanding eyes and explosion to drive downhill (22.0 tackles for loss in 2021) and the athleticism to make plays in coverage (four interceptions, two pick-sixes in 2021).

10 New York Jets (from Seattle)
Garrett Wilson, WR, Ohio State

With all due respect to Jamison Crowder and Braxton Berrios, when they are your most productive pass-catchers, you officially have a wide receiver problem. Quarterback Zach Wilson must show improvements in year two, but he also needs the front office to find him more help.

I have six wide receivers ranked as top-25 prospects in this class, with Wilson as the clear No. 1 guy. He has only average size (6-0, 186), but he is a three-level threat due to his athleticism and ball skills. What separates him the most is his ability to create space before and after the catch.

11 Washington Commanders
Kenny Pickett, QB, Pittsburgh

Washington has a poor track record of drafting quarterbacks in the early rounds. Since the merger in 1970, the franchise has drafted eight quarterbacks in the top 100 picks, and only one (Jay Schroeder) of the eight had a winning record with the organization. That means Washington is due, right? Pickett doesn't have an explosive arm, but he is accurate from various platforms and his football IQ makes him NFL ready.

12 Minnesota Vikings
Ahmad Gardner, CB, Cincinnati

Opinions are split around the league if Gardner belongs in the top-15 or if he should come off the board in the back-half of round one. The Cincinnati corner was a three-year starter and didn't give up a touchdown in over 1,100 coverage snaps in college. Gardner gets a little handsy, but he has the long-striding speed and hip-flip to stay on top of routes.

13 Cleveland Browns
Treylon Burks, WR, Arkansas

The Browns passing offense desperately needs another playmaker and Burks has the ability to create big plays. He has an outstanding blend of size (6-3, 228) and speed (4.45) with the tracking skills and catch radius to be a quarterback's best friend. Burks, who led the SEC with 22 plays of 20-plus yards in 2021, reminds me of a linebacker-sized Deebo Samuel.

14 Baltimore Ravens
Travon Walker, DL, Georgia

Good players just seem to fall to the Ravens in the draft, right? That is the case here because it wouldn't surprise me if Walker ends up being one of the best defensive players from this draft class. With players like Calais Campbell and Brandon Williams set to hit free agency, the Ravens' defensive line could look very different in 2022.

15 Philadelphia Eagles (from Miami)
Tyler Linderbaum, OC, Iowa

Obviously, this selection is based on the future of Jason Kelce, who just earned his fourth All-Pro nod. Even if he returns for his age 35 season in 2022, Kelce would be the ideal mentor for Linderbaum, who has exceptional quickness and a nasty streak to dominate defenders.

16 Philadelphia Eagles (from Indianapolis)
Andrew Booth Jr., CB, Clemson

With Steven Nelson headed for free agency, cornerback could be a need for the Eagles this offseason. Booth is a terrific athlete and can make plays on the ball — the two most important traits when scouting the position. Booth also has above-average downhill skills to drive and blow up plays near the line of scrimmage.

17 Los Angeles Chargers
Trevor Penning, OT, Northern Iowa

Do the Chargers make the playoffs if they receive better play at right tackle over the final month of the season? Penning has a massive frame (6-7, 329, 35-inch arms) with the athletic footwork and competitive chops to develop into a Pro Bowl-level player.

18 New Orleans Saints
Matt Corral, QB, Ole Miss

The Saints are in limbo with their quarterback situation, but Corral could be the answer that new head coach Dennis Allen needs. The Ole Miss quarterback has the athleticism of Taysom Hill coupled with an explosive arm and passing instincts to create big plays through the air.

19 Philadelphia Eagles
George Karlaftis, edge, Purdue

The Eagles' defensive end depth chart will likely look wildly different next season, and Karlaftis would be a welcomed addition. The Purdue pass rusher doesn't have elite length or twitch, but he is relentless and strong with hand work that is not only violent but also well-timed and strategic to defeat blockers.

20 Pittsburgh Steelers
Sam Howell, QB, North Carolina

With Ben Roethlisberger having played his final game in a Steelers' uniform, there is a "Quarterback Wanted" sign hanging on the front of Heinz Field. Although Howell's junior season didn't go exactly according to plan, he has NFL-level arm talent and mobility and is ready to step in as the Steelers' starter from day one.

21 New England Patriots
Nakobe Dean, LB, Georgia

Generally, Bill Belichick prefers bigger-bodied linebackers, but what Dean lacks in size he more than makes up for with play speed and football smarts. And anyone who watched the Patriots' playoff loss to the Bills knows they need more of both at linebacker.

22 Las Vegas Raiders
Drake London, WR, USC

Derek Carr was playing well enough for the Raiders to make a postseason run, but he needed another playmaker in the playoff loss to the Bengals. London, who was averaging 11 catches and 135.5 yards per game before his injury, has the basketball athleticism to play above the rim and be a chain-mover.

23 Arizona Cardinals
Jordan Davis, DT, Georgia

At 6-6 and 360 pounds, Davis is a hard-to-move space-eater with the power to reestablish the line of scrimmage. He might be drafted higher if a team believes he can sustain his high level of play with an increased snap count (he averaged only 25.2 snaps per game in 2021), but Davis is a dominant run defender when on the field.

24 Dallas Cowboys
Kenyon Green, OG, Texas A&M

Left guard Connor Williams, who has probably played his final game in Dallas, was a liability for most of the Cowboys' wild-card game, and the 49ers took advantage. Although Green played predominantly at left guard for the Aggies, he also logged starts at left tackle, right tackle and right guard in 2021 and would give Dallas a versatile blocker who can fill in at several positions if needed.

25 Buffalo Bills
Jameson Williams, WR, Alabama

Giving a weapon like Williams to Josh Allen and the Bills' offense hardly seems fair. Wide receiver isn't at the top of the Bills' needs, but it would be tough to pass on Williams' talent if he were to fall this far due to his recent torn ACL. Teams will have more information about his knee and surgery at the scouting combine.

26 Tennessee Titans
Jahan Dotson, WR, Penn State

With his twitchy athleticism and route-running skills, Dotson consistently puts cornerbacks in conflict. Although he is undersized and won't break many tackles, he has the dynamic speed and ball skills that will give the Titans another dimension on offense.

27 Tampa Bay Buccaneers
Logan Hall, DL, Houston

Hall is one of the more underrated prospects in this draft class, and I wouldn't be surprised if he is long gone by this pick. Personally, I like him best as an edge rusher where he has a little bit of a runway and can unlock his quickness and length. But Hall would give Tampa flexibility on the defensive line as Houston head coach Dana Holgorsen has called him "one of the best" defensive tackles he has ever coached.

28 Green Bay Packers
DeMarvin Leal, DL, Texas A&M

The Packers love toolsy front-seven defenders, and Leal is exactly that. He isn't yet the sum of his parts, which is why he could still be available at this point in the first round. But at 6-4 and 290 pounds, Leal can line up anywhere on the defensive line and has the traits to develop into a productive starter.

29 Miami Dolphins (from San Francisco)
Jermaine Johnson, edge, Florida State

The Dolphins drafted an edge rusher in the first round last year but could do it again with Emmanuel Ogbah a free agent. Johnson has the length, agility and violent hands to be disruptive as both a pass rusher and run defender.

30 Kansas City Chiefs
Daxton Hill, CB/FS, Michigan

With Tyrann Mathieu, Charvarius Ward and Mike Hughes all free agents, the Chiefs' secondary figures to look a little different next season regardless of the team's draft strategy. Hill is not only an option at safety, but he played a slot cornerback role for the Wolverines and can do the same in Kansas City, which would allow L'Jarius Sneed to play outside full-time.

31 Cincinnati Bengals
Trent McDuffie, CB, Washington

Maybe this is an overreaction to watching Vernon Hargreaves trying to cover the Raiders, but cornerback could be in the mix here. McDuffie doesn't have great ball production, but there weren't many opportunities because he prevents throws by blanketing his side of the field.

32 Detroit Lions (from Los Angeles)
Chris Olave, WR, Ohio State

I don't think the Lions will feel pressured to take a wide receiver here, especially with the emergence of Amon-Ra St. Brown over the final month of the season. But Olave and his polished play style would give Detroit an immediate playmaker for an offense in need of them.

Second Round

No.	Team	Player
33	Jacksonville Jaguars	Kaiir Elam, CB, Florida
34	Detroit Lions	Roger McCreary, CB, Auburn
35	New York Jets	Bernhard Raimann, OT/G, Central Michigan
36	New York Giants	Desmond Ridder, QB, Cincinnati
37	Houston Texans	Kenneth Walker, RB, Michigan State
38	New York Jets (from Carolina)	Trey McBride, TE, Colorado State
39	Chicago Bears	George Pickens, WR, Georgia
40	Denver Broncos	Myjai Sanders, edge, Cincinnati
41	Seattle Seahawks	Daniel Faalele, OT, Minnesota
42	Washington Commanders	Darian Kinnard, OT/G, Kentucky
43	Atlanta Falcons	Malik Willis, QB, Liberty
44	Cleveland Browns	Drake Jackson, edge, USC
45	Baltimore Ravens	Nicholas Petit-Frere, OT, Ohio State
46	Minnesota Vikings	Kingsley Enagbare, edge, South Carolina
47	Indianapolis Colts	Carson Strong, QB, Nevada

No.	Team	Player
48	Los Angeles Chargers	Phidarian Mathis, DT, Alabama
49	New Orleans Saints	Jalen Tolbert, WR, South Alabama
50	Miami Dolphins	Damone Clark, LB, LSU
51	Philadelphia Eagles	Chad Muma, LB, Wyoming
52	Pittsburgh Steelers	Zion Johnson, OG, Boston College
53	Las Vegas Raiders	Christian Harris, LB, Alabama
54	New England Patriots	John Metchie, WR, Alabama
55	Arizona Cardinals	Cameron Thomas, edge, San Diego State
56	Dallas Cowboys	Jaquan Brisker, DS, Penn State
57	Buffalo Bills	Sean Rhyan, OG, UCLA
58	Atlanta Falcons (from Tennessee)	David Bell, WR, Purdue
59	Tampa Bay Buccaneers	Breece Hall, RB, Iowa State
60	Green Bay Packers	Jeremy Ruckert, TE, Ohio State
61	San Francisco 49ers	Lewis Cine, DS, Georgia
62	Kansas City Chiefs	Arnold Ebiketie, edge, Penn State
63	Cincinnati Bengals	Rasheed Walker, OT, Penn State
64	Denver Broncos (from Los Angeles)	Marcus Jones, CB, Houston

Dane Brugler's 2022 NFL Draft Position Rankings

Michigan pass rushers
Aidan Hutchinson and
David Ojabo ascending

Quarterbacks

1 Kenny Pickett
Pittsburgh (6-3, 217 pounds)

Pickett is a testament to betting on yourself and constantly improving, which makes him a throwback of sorts. He opted in for a fifth season, taking advantage of the NCAA's bonus COVID-19 year, and turned into one of the best players in the country, completing 67 percent of his passes for 4,319 yards with 42 touchdowns and seven interceptions, plus five rushing touchdowns. He broke multiple Pitt records that had been set by Dan Marino, and he finished third in the Heisman Trophy voting. – **Matt Fortuna**

2 Malik Willis
Liberty (6-0, 220)

The Atlanta native had a rocky start to his college career at Auburn but left the Plains and flourished in Hugh Freeze's system, relying on his powerful arm and dynamic running ability. The buzz around Willis shot up in 2020 after he led the Flames to wins over Syracuse and Virginia Tech, then ran for 137 yards and four touchdowns in a bowl win over No. 12 Coastal Carolina. In 2021, he had some consistency issues, though, with three three-interception games. He also was very shaky in a blowout loss against Louisiana, where he went just 14-of-34. – Bruce Feldman

3 Matt Corral
Ole Miss (6-2, 205)

Corral's ability has never been questioned. Recruiting observers said he had one of the best arms to come out of the West Coast in recent memory. Corral had an odd recruiting journey and a bumpy start to his career, but he harnessed all of that ability under Lane Kiffin's tutelage and became one of the best quarterbacks in the country. Corral was the face of Ole Miss' resurgence and carried the offense, passing for 6,686 yards and 49 touchdowns (with 19 interceptions) and rushing for 1,120 yards and 15 touchdowns over the past two seasons. – Antonio Morales

4 Sam Howell
North Carolina (6-0, 221)

Howell ended his three-year career with North Carolina as one of the most productive quarterbacks in ACC history. The Indian Trail, N.C., native threw for 10,283 career passing yards — fifth-most in ACC history — and 92 passing touchdowns, third-most in league history. A Day 1 starter, Howell set 27 UNC records, including career marks for passing yards, passing yards per game, passing efficiency and total offense. The Tar Heels' record didn't do him any favors, but there's no denying Howell enters the NFL as one of the program's most prolific players ever. – Grace Raynor

Desmond Ridder
Cincinnati (6-3, 207)

It took Ridder less than one quarter of the 2018 season opener to earn the starting job for the Bearcats as a redshirt freshman. Over the next four seasons, he evolved from mainly a running threat to an all-around dual-threat quarterback, improving his accuracy, defensive recognition and deep ball, all on his way to becoming one of the top-five winningest quarterbacks in college football history and leading Cincinnati on a historic Playoff run in 2021. His passing precision and decision making still need refining, but his raw abilities are ideal for the new wave of NFL quarterbacks. – Justin Williams

 Carson Strong
Nevada (6-4, 226)

Despite his large frame and big arm, Strong was overlooked coming out of high school in Northern California. Nevada was his only FBS offer, but he quickly emerged as a perfect fit for the Air Raid offense. He completed 70 percent of his passes in each of the past two years with more than eight yards per attempt and 335 passing yards per game, as Nevada had its most successful run since the days of Colin Kaepernick. He can make every throw, but a lingering knee issue from high school caused him to miss fall camp this past season. – Chris Vannini

Bailey Zappe
Western Kentucky (6-0, 213)

After passing for more than 10,000 yards over four seasons at Houston Baptist, Zappe bet on himself and moved up to the FBS level with his OC Zach Kittley. Zappe proved he was the real deal at Western Kentucky, breaking FBS single-season records for passing yards (5,967) and passing touchdowns (62) in the Hilltoppers' thrilling Air Raid attack. He guided them to wins in eight of their last nine games and played for the Conference USA title. Zappe's coaches love his competitiveness, high football IQ and accuracy and are confident those traits will translate in the NFL. – Max Olson

8 Jack Coan
Notre Dame (6-3, 223)

Coan arrived at Notre Dame with a "game manager" label, struggled to even be that at first, then departed as better than advertised after his graduate transfer from Wisconsin. Working behind a poor offensive line highlighted Coan's lack of mobility, but it also made him speed up his decision making during the second half of the Irish's season. The results were good enough that offensive coordinator Tommy Rees built the entire Fiesta Bowl game plan around Coan, who went 38 of 68 for 509 yards and five touchdowns against Oklahoma State. Rees predicted Coan would be an NFL quarterback before the season ended. He might be right. – Pete Sampson

9 Kaleb Eleby
Western Michigan (6-1, 216)

Eleby came out of nowhere to lead the nation in yards per attempt (11.2) in a six-game MAC-only season in 2020, after redshirting in 2019. He had an up-and-down 2021: He threw for 337 yards and three touchdowns in a win at ACC champion Pitt, probably the best game of his career, but he also struggled against Michigan and some MAC opponents. He took care of the ball, throwing 45 touchdowns to 11 interceptions over 24 starts, and he threw multiple interceptions in a game just twice. – Chris Vannini

10 Cole Kelley
Southeastern Louisiana (6-7, 250)

Kelley went to Arkansas out of high school and became an SEC starter as a true freshman, but an up-and-down road led him to transfer to Southeastern Louisiana. That's where Kelley proved himself, breaking out in 2020-21 and winning the Walter Payton Award for top offensive player with 2,662 yards and 18 touchdowns in seven games. The imposing quarterback followed it up with 5,124 yards and 44 touchdowns this fall. – Brody Miller

11 EJ Perry
Brown (6-1, 200)

After backing up Anthony Brown for two years at Boston College, Perry transferred to play for his uncle at Brown. He was ready for his shot to shine and set a new Ivy League record for total offense (3,678 yards) in 2019. Perry had to wait a year to follow that up – Brown did not play in 2020 – and was excellent yet again, winning Ivy League Offensive Player of the Year as a senior. He got scouts' attention at the East-West Shrine Bowl by passing for 241 yards and three TDs to earn offensive MVP honors. – Max Olson

12 Brock Purdy
Iowa State (6-1, 216)

Purdy's status as Iowa State's greatest quarterback is virtually unchallenged. He led seven fourth-quarter comebacks and engineered seven wins against ranked opponents. With a 30-17 record, Purdy owns 32 school records and was a four-time All-Big 12 selection, including first-team honors in 2020 when he led ISU to its first Big 12 title game appearance. Last year, Purdy led the Big 12 in passing yards per game (245.2) and ranked fifth nationally in completion percentage (71.7). He finished his college career with 81 touchdown passes, 12,170 passing yards and 1,177 rushing yards. – Scott Dochterman

13 Skylar Thompson
Kansas State (6-2, 224)

Thompson's leadership and toughness always impressed in his six years at Kansas State. He started 40 games for the Wildcats, led them to big wins and three bowl games and is the first QB in school history to finish with more than 7,000 passing yards plus 1,000 rushing yards in his career. Thompson had to come back from shoulder and knee injuries in his final two years but still put together his most efficient season yet as a senior. – Max Olson

14 Dustin Crum
Kent State (6-1, 210)

The former two-star recruit from Grafton, Ohio, started 30 games over his final three seasons and left Kent State as the school's second all-time leading passer, completing 66.7 percent of his 864 attempts for 7,420 yards, 55 touchdowns and only 12 interceptions while also running for 2,071 yards and 24 scores on 477 attempts. Kent State hasn't had a player drafted to play quarterback in the NFL since Greg Kokal in 1976. Crum was named the MAC Offensive Player of the Year in 2021. – Manny Navarro

15 Aqeel Glass
Alabama A&M (6-4, 228)

Glass was one of the most prolific passers in FCS history at Alabama A&M, finishing with 12,136 passing yards (fourth-most in SWAC history) and 109 touchdowns. He won the Deacon Jones Trophy, awarded to the most outstanding HBCU player, in the 2021 spring season after his undefeated Bulldogs were named HBCU national champs. He won it again in the fall, too, and was once against SWAC Offensive Player of the Year after throwing for more than 350 yards per game. Glass is hoping to become the first HBCU quarterback selected in the draft since Tarvaris Jackson in 2006. – Max Olson

Running Backs

1 Kenneth Walker III
Michigan State (5-10, 212 pounds)

Walker was only at Michigan State for a year, but he parlayed it into one of the more impressive individual seasons in school history. Walker rushed for 1,636 yards (fourth all-time at MSU) and 18 touchdowns in 2021, earning consensus first-team All-America honors, the Doak Walker Award and the Walter Camp Award in the process. He led all Power 5 running backs in yards after contact (1,168) and was the driving force behind Michigan State's 11-2 turnaround season. His contributions won't soon be forgotten in East Lansing. – **Colton Pouncy**

2 Isaiah Spiller
Texas A&M (6-1, 215)

Spiller may have been one of college football's most underappreciated players during his career. A reliable, consistent back, he finished just seven yards shy of 3,000 career rushing yards in three seasons. His patience, vision and cutting ability led to productivity in traffic, even when his offensive line was underwhelming. His disciplined nature made negative plays a rarity. He was also an impactful, dependable receiver out of the backfield, catching 74 passes in his career. A leader on and off the field, Spiller handled himself like a pro while at A&M and was a model teammate. – Sam Khan Jr.

3 Breece Hall
Iowa State (6-1, 220)

Hall was an all-time great for Iowa State, a two-time All-American and Big 12 Offensive Player of the Year who was often dominant but always consistent. He averaged 143.5 total yards per game after earning the starting job during his freshman season and set a new NCAA record with rushing touchdowns in 24 consecutive games. Hall helped lead the Cyclones to new heights, including their first Big 12 title game in 2020, and demonstrated he has all the tools to be a reliable, dangerous back at the next level. – Max Olson

4 Tyler Allgeier
BYU (5-11, 221)

Allgeier's ascent as a one-time walk-on running back to starting linebacker and back to running back was astonishing. Once he established himself as the starter in 2019, Allgeier went on to break several records at BYU, most recently the single-season rushing record with 1,601 yards in 2021. He also was tied for the most rushing touchdowns in the country last year with 23. Allgeier only garnered more power in the run game as games wore on, routinely punishing opposing defensive lines with his blend of power and deceptive speed. – Christopher Kamrani

5 Kyren Williams
Notre Dame (5-9, 199)

The heartbeat of Notre Dame's offense and arguably the entire program, Williams rushed for 1,002 yards in 2021 in spite of a woeful offensive line, with more than three quarters of his rushing production coming after contact. He was also an outstanding asset in pass protection, with his skills as a receiver growing through his junior year. His 42 receptions were third on the team. Williams took the fuzzy intangibles of drive, heart and toughness, then turned them into assets for Notre Dame. He's the first Notre Dame running back to post back-to-back 1,000-yard seasons since Darius Walker in 2005-06. – Pete Sampson

6 Dameon Pierce
Florida (5-9, 220)

A top-10 all-time rusher in Georgia high school history with 6,779 yards, Pierce started 11 games for the Gators over his final two years but was never given a heavy enough workload (his career-high was 15 carries against Georgia in 2021) to climb up Florida's all-time rushing list. He averaged 5.5 yards per carry on 329 attempts with 23 touchdowns and was ranked the third-most elusive Power 5 back with at least 100 carries in 2021 by Pro Football Focus. He forced 49 missed tackles on 119 touches. Pierce had 45 career catches for 422 yards and five scores as a receiver. – Manny Navarro

7 James Cook
Georgia (5-11, 195)

Previous offensive coordinators didn't find a way to use Cook's explosive abilities, but once Todd Monken arrived at Georgia in 2020 – and D'Andre Swift turned pro – Cook was turned loose as both a runner and receiver. He was Georgia's leader in combined rushing and receiving yards in 2021 (728 rushing and 284 receiving), and he led the Bulldogs' tailbacks in total snaps. Cook was dangerous when he got the ball in space but also able to get yardage on traditional run plays. – Seth Emerson

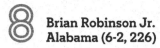

Brian Robinson Jr.
Alabama (6-2, 226)

Robinson was the rare fifth-year college running back, but that fifth year was vital to raising his profile after sitting behind players like Najee Harris, Josh Jacobs and Damien Harris. Robinson's style is all about toughness. He's a one-cut back who does his best running going north and south. He had his best season in 2021 with 1,343 rushing yards and 14 touchdowns while averaging 8.5 yards per catch and two touchdowns. – Aaron Suttles

Hassan Haskins
Michigan (6-0, 220)

Haskins was buried on the depth chart early in his Michigan career and briefly switched to linebacker before giving running back another shot. When he finally got his chance midway through the 2019 season, Haskins immediately became Michigan's most productive running back. He finished his career with 2,324 rushing yards and 30 touchdowns, including a school-record 20 as a senior. Haskins is a powerful runner and a deceptively talented athlete who makes the most of every carry. – Austin Meek

Zonovan Knight
NC State (5-11, 210)

Knight is an all-purpose running back who can contribute to an NFL team both in the backfield and as an electric kick returner. He earned first-team All-ACC honors as a specialist in 2021 thanks to two 100-yard kickoff returns, and he holds NC State's career record with 35.2 yards per kickoff return. Knight also finished his career ranked 12th in program history in rushing yards with 2,286 yards on 419 carries and tied for 14th in rushing touchdowns. His 5.46 yards per carry are also a school record. – Grace Raynor

11   Zamir White
Georgia (6-0, 215)

White had a rough start to his career: The five-star recruit tore his ACL twice, first in a high school all-star game and then during a Georgia practice. He worked his way back to become Georgia's starting tailback and leading rusher the past two seasons. While his reputation was as the more traditional, between-the-tackles runner, he was occasionally involved in the passing game and broke a few runs to the edge. The further away he got from the second ACL injury, the more confident and (occasionally) explosive he became. – Seth Emerson

12   Abram Smith
Baylor (5-11, 211)

Although he was recruited as a running back, Smith took a winding path back to the position at Baylor. After playing mostly as a special teams contributor in his first two years, Smith excelled as a linebacker in 2020, starting four times for injured teammate Terrel Bernard. He returned to running back in 2021 when new offensive coordinator Jeff Grimes sought a downhill runner for his wide zone-heavy scheme. Smith's tough, bruising style made him a perfect fit. He led the Big 12 in rushing yards (1,601), hitting the century mark nine times. He was the heart and soul of Baylor's 2021 offense. – Sam Khan Jr.

13   Jerome Ford
Cincinnati (5-11, 209)

The Alabama transfer running back grew tired of that moniker by the end of his second season with the Bearcats, but it's a convenient shorthand for the talent level he brought to Cincinnati and will take to the next level. Ford has an ideal frame for an NFL running back to pair with impressive vision and breakaway speed, as evidenced by the 1,319 rushing yards, 6.1 yards per carry and 20 total touchdowns he racked up in 2021, including 10 runs of 20-plus yards. – Justin Williams

14 Tyler Badie
Missouri (5-8, 199)

In a conference that has no shortage of talent, Badie flourished in the SEC. The New Orleans native led the conference and ranked third nationally in 2021 in rushing yards per game with 133.7. He also finished fourth nationally in total rushing yards with 1,604. In his final year in Columbia, he showed what he could do in the passing game, as well. Ten catches for 88 yards and a touchdown against Kentucky in Week 2 and eight catches for 40 yards against Vanderbilt in October suggest he can do a little bit of everything at the next level.
– Grace Raynor

15 D'Vonte Price
Florida International (6-1, 198)

A downhill runner, Price (6-2, 215) averaged six yards per carry, had eight 100-yard rushing performances and totaled 2,203 yards and 16 touchdowns on 369 carries over his 46-game career. His 6.84 yards per carry in 2020 set a school record and earned him All-Conference USA honorable mention. The Punta Gorda (Fla.) native produced 422 of his 674 yards rushing in 2021 after contact, according to Pro Football Focus. He still has a lot to prove as a receiver, though: In his career, he had 45 catches for 307 yards and a score. FIU has never had a running back drafted. – Manny Navarro

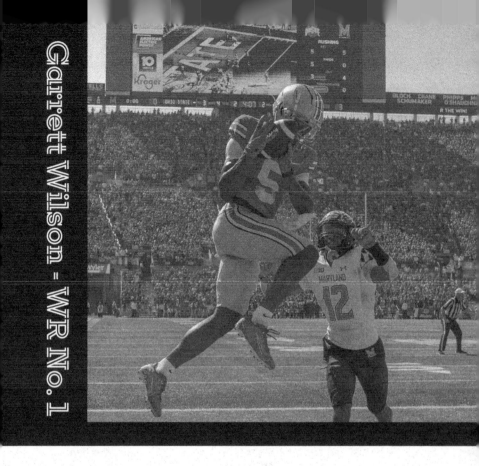

Wide Receivers

1 Garrett Wilson
Ohio State (6-0, 186 pounds)

Wilson had the perfect Ohio State career in that he was recruited out of Texas as a highly regarded five-star prospect, made an immediate impact and left three years later as one of the most explosive and productive receivers the program has ever seen. You could argue that Wilson's arrival in Columbus kicked off the run of elite receiver talent flowing through the program under receivers coach Brian Hartline. Wilson and Chris Olave formed one of the best receiver tandems in the country for two seasons. Wilson finished his career at Ohio State top-10 in receptions, yards and touchdowns. – **Bill Landis**

2 Treylon Burks
Arkansas (6-3, 232)

Burks' combination of size and speed meant big production at Arkansas and positions him as a versatile weapon and red zone target at the next level. He spent some time in the Razorbacks' backfield a la Deebo Samuel, but his biggest asset is hauling in contested catches. That size also allows him to break tackles, and he's a proven playmaker who can turn short gains into big gains when he's isolated against defensive backs in space. – David Ubben

3 Drake London
USC (6-5, 212)

London came to USC as a relatively under-the-radar prospect, but he broke out midway through his freshman year and from there became one of the most impressive receivers the Trojans have had in recent memory, which is saying something considering the talent they've had at the position. London utilizes his frame and basketball background to dominate in contested-catch situations and generate highlight plays. He caught 88 passes for 1,084 yards and seven touchdowns in 2021 and was named Pac-12 Offensive Player of the Year despite missing the final four games of the season with a fractured ankle. – Antonio Morales

4 Jameson Williams
Alabama (6-2, 182)

The argument could be made that no player has taken better advantage of the transfer portal than Williams. A backup at Ohio State, Williams became one of the nation's best wide receivers after transferring to Alabama. Initially thought of as only a speed receiver, Williams showed his other skills in a dominant junior season. His knee injury in the national championship game is a setback, but it's not expected to affect his career that much. His speed will have NFL teams very intrigued. – Aaron Suttles

5 Chris Olave
Ohio State (6-1, 182)

An unsung and under-the-radar member of OSU's 2018 recruiting class, Olave blossomed into one of the best to ever play the receiver position in Columbus. He burst onto the scene with a couple of touchdowns and a blocked punt against Michigan as a true freshman and never looked back. He finished his career top-five in program history in receptions and yards, and No. 1 in touchdowns. In addition to that, he was a key special teams starter for four seasons. – Bill Landis

6 Jahan Dotson
Penn State (5-11, 175)

Penn State's do-it-all receiver and punt returner the last two seasons, Dotson made countless acrobatic catches while dealing with inconsistent quarterback play and struggling offenses around him. He was the player Penn State game-planned to get the ball to as often as possible, and still he was only rarely bottled up. As a junior, the surehanded Dotson averaged a whopping 17 yards per reception during the Big Ten's shortened nine-game season. As a senior he torched defenses, finishing with 91 receptions for 1,182 yards and 12 touchdowns in 12 games. – Audrey Snyder

7 Jalen Tolbert
South Alabama (6-1, 195)

Tolbert improved with each season at South Alabama and became unstoppable in the Sun Belt in his fourth and final season, with 82 catches for 1,474 yards and eight touchdowns. He had seven 100-yard performances in 12 games, including 143 yards against Sun Belt champion Louisiana and 10 catches for 191 yards against Coastal Carolina. A big-play threat, Tolbert led the nation in catches of 30-plus yards and 40-plus yards, consistently making difficult plays. – Chris Vannini

8 John Metchie III
Alabama (5-11, 196)

Metchie was the meat and potatoes of the Alabama offense. While Jameson Williams provided the flash, Metchie worked underneath and shined as a more experienced route runner – look no further than his game-winning overtime reception against Auburn, when he beat highly touted corner Roger McCreary on the route easily. Metchie is coming off a knee injury he sustained in the SEC championship game, but he is expected to make a full recovery. – Aaron Suttles

9 George Pickens
Georgia (6-3, 203)

Pickens was an electric talent the minute he arrived at Georgia, when a scrimmage highlight of him making a one-handed sideline grab went viral. There was more of that when he was on the field, including a diving catch in this year's national championship. The trick was being on the field: Pickens first had minor issues with behavior, like squirting an opponent with a water bottle, and had a couple of small suspensions as a freshman. Then he tore his ACL in 2021 spring practice, but he worked his way back to be with the team during the run to the title. – Seth Emerson

10 David Bell
Purdue (6-2, 207)

Over the last three seasons, no receiver has caught more passes than Bell's 232. A first-team All-American in 2021, Bell totaled 2,946 yards in 29 career games and combined a savvy ability to get open with uncommon strength to break away from defenders. According to PFF, Bell forced 25 missed tackles after the catch, which led the nation in 2021. He also paced the nation in yards after the catch and after contact. This year in a win over No. 2 Iowa, Bell caught 11 passes for 240 yards. Against No. 3 Michigan State three weeks later, he grabbed 11 passes for 217 yards. – Scott Dochterman

11 Wan'Dale Robinson
Kentucky (5-10, 187)

Mr. Football in Kentucky in 2019, Robinson followed Scott Frost to Nebraska out of high school because he worried about UK's run-first offense. Then Frost used Robinson heavily at running back for two seasons. He had more carries (134) than catches (91) as a Cornhusker. When Mark Stoops plucked Liam Coen from the Sean McVay coaching tree and brought the Rams' offense to Lexington last season, Robinson came home to play in that NFL system. The result: He set single-season records at Kentucky for catches (104) and receiving yards (1,334) and ranked eighth nationally in scrimmage plays of 30-plus yards (13). He won Citrus Bowl MVP with 10 catches for 170 yards — also UK records — against Iowa. – Kyle Tucker

12 Skyy Moore
Western Michigan (5-9, 195)

Moore averaged 107.8 receiving yards per game in 2021, good for second in his conference and eighth in the country. His 10 touchdowns also ranked tied for first in the MAC. With two years of eligibility remaining, Moore should enter the NFL Draft fresh and with plenty of tread left on the tires for his next team. In 2019, he became the first true freshman wide receiver to earn All-MAC honors in program history. – Grace Raynor

13 Justyn Ross
Clemson (6-4, 209)

Ross didn't know if he'd ever play football again after he learned in the spring of 2020 that he had a congenital fusion in his spine. But he returned to the field in 2021 and finished his Clemson career tied for fifth in program history with 20 touchdown receptions. Although his 2021 numbers were down as Clemson's offense sputtered, Ross still caught 158 career passes for 2,379 yards. He led Clemson in receiving as a freshman with 1,000 yards despite never starting a game and dazzled in the 2018 national championship with six catches for 153 yards and a touchdown. – Grace Raynor

14   Christian Watson
North Dakota State (6-4, 211)

Watson's frame is the first thing that stands out. He averaged a whopping 20.4 yards per catch for his career, which included 21.5 yards per catch in 2019 and 23.3 yards per catch in 2020. He also can help an NFL team on special teams, having finished fourth in program history with 26.4 career yards per kickoff return. Although Watson played at the FCS level, he's no stranger to the spotlight. He earned FCS All-American honors twice and was part of four national championship teams in his five years at North Dakota State. – Grace Raynor

15   Alec Pierce
Cincinnati (6-3, 208)

His size gives the impression of an old-school, big-bodied receiver, but Pierce pairs it with sub-4.5 speed and a 40-inch vertical. He was largely an over-the-top deep threat early in his college career — and he maintained that capability with 11 receptions for 25-plus yards in 2021 — but he really developed his route running and all-around skills as a receiver, including as a stellar blocker on the edge in the run game. He hauled in 52 catches for 884 yards and eight touchdowns in 2021. – Justin Williams

Tight Ends

1 Trey McBride
Colorado State (6-3, 249 pounds)

McBride won the 2021 Mackey Award as college football's top tight end. His 90 catches in 2021 were nearly 20 more than any other tight end in FBS and more than double any other Rams player. McBride carried the offense for a struggling Colorado State team, and only one of those 90 catches resulted in a touchdown. He finished his career with 164 catches for 2,100 yards, making him a consistent weapon in the passing game. – Chris Vannini

2 Jeremy Ruckert
Ohio State (6-5, 250)

Ruckert was a borderline five-star prospect coming out of high school but probably never got the receiver work most expected for a player of his caliber. However, when his number was called, Ruckert usually delivered. He's likely to be more of a receiver threat in the NFL than he was in college, but his four seasons in Columbus saw him develop physically into a more well-rounded tight end. – Bill Landis

3 Isaiah Likely
Coastal Carolina (6-4, 241)

Look no further than Likely's performance against Arkansas State on Oct. 7 to understand what kind of pass-catching tight end he can be in the NFL. That day he set new Sun Belt and Coastal Carolina records when he caught eight passes for 232 yards and four touchdowns. He finished his final season at Coastal Carolina as the Sun Belt's third-leading receiver with 59 catches for 912 yards and a league-high 12 touchdowns. It's no wonder he was a semifinalist for the Mackey Award. – Grace Raynor

4 Greg Dulcich
UCLA (6-4, 248)

Dulcich began his collegiate career as a walk-on and turned into a big-play threat by the end of his time at UCLA. Dulcich caught 42 passes for 725 yards and five touchdowns in 2021, averaging 17.5 yards per reception. He's an explosive target in the pass game and is tough to tackle in yards-after-catch opportunities. Dulcich was first-team All-Pac-12 and a semifinalist for the Mackey Award. – Antonio Morales

5 Cade Otton
Washington (6-5, 240)

After establishing himself as a willing blocker early in his career, Otton developed into one of Washington's primary receiving threats in his final two seasons. Though his 2021 season was shortened by COVID-19 protocols and injury — and thwarted, too, by an anemic offense that precipitated a coordinator firing — Otton still finished third on the team in receptions after leading the team in targets, catches, yards and touchdowns in 2020. He's a well-rounded tight end with ideal size to hold up in the NFL, similar to former UW teammate Drew Sample. – Christian Caple

6 Jalen Wydermyer
Texas A&M (6-5, 255)

Wydermyer contributed from the moment he stepped on campus. He shined as a true freshman in 2019 and was a Mackey Award finalist and All-SEC pick in 2020 and 2021. He thrived in Jimbo Fisher's tight end-friendly offense, catching 118 passes for 1,468 yards and 16 touchdowns. His size and speed consistently gave opposing defenses problems. His sophomore season, which included a team-high 46 catches, was his best. Though he was similarly productive as a junior, drops became an issue (his eight in 2021 were highest among FBS tight ends, per Pro Football Focus). – Sam Khan Jr.

7 Charlie Kolar
Iowa State (6-6, 256)

Few players in this draft have a more impressive college résumé than Kolar. He's a three-time All-American and two-time Mackey Award finalist who finished in the top five in receiving yards among tight ends for three consecutive years and broke every school record for his position. He was an invaluable weapon in the passing game who gained first downs on 70 percent of his career catches. Kolar also earned the prestigious William V. Campbell Trophy, considered the Heisman of academics, and was a three-time Academic All-American as a 3.99 GPA student with a mechanical engineering degree. – Max Olson

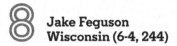

8 Jake Feguson
Wisconsin (6-4, 244)

Ferguson was a consistent performer for four seasons at Wisconsin who finished his career with 145 receptions for 1,618 yards and 13 touchdowns. He caught at least one pass in all 47 games in which he played. He excelled with his athleticism and body control in a big frame, which allowed him to adjust to the ball in the air and make contested catches. Ferguson was a workhorse who played 2,637 career snaps, including 1,450 as a run blocker, per Pro Football Focus, which means he has as much experience as any tight end in the draft. – Jesse Temple

9 Cole Turner
Nevada (6-6, 246)

Turner came to Nevada as a wide receiver but transitioned to tight end in the second half of his career, adding bulk to fill out his frame (he was 193 pounds coming out of high school). He grabbed 111 catches for 1,282 yards and 19 touchdowns over the last two seasons, twice earning all-conference honors, as he created all kinds of mismatches in Nevada's Air Raid offense. He missed a game in 2021 due to a concussion but did return. His best game was a 12-catch, 175-yard performance against Hawaii in 2021. – Chris Vannini

10 Jelani Woods
Virginia (6-7, 275)

Woods has tremendous size at the tight end position and uses it to his advantage. After being underused as a passing target at Oklahoma State, he thrived in one year with the Cavaliers, catching 44 passes for 598 yards and eight touchdowns, eclipsing his combined totals from the previous three years in each category. He won't give you a ton of yards after the catch, but he's a big target, particularly in the red zone. – Andy Bitter

11 Daniel Bellinger
San Diego State (6-6, 250)

San Diego State's passing offense wasn't prolific by any stretch of the imagination, but Bellinger made the most of his limited opportunities. He caught 31 passes for 357 yards in 2021, which was good for third on the team, and two scores, nearly matching his combined reception total from the past two seasons (36). Bellinger was also heavily involved in the Aztecs' run game as a blocker and benefited from the open opportunities it created in the play-action pass game. – Antonio Morales

12 John FitzPatrick
Georgia (6-6, 250)

FitzPatrick's stats may not be gaudy (16 career catches for 172 yards and one TD), but he was a key part of the Georgia offense the past two years, drawing a number of snaps in an offense that liberally used multiple-tight end sets. FitzPatrick was a dependable blocker on run and pass plays and would have drawn more targets if not for the presence of Tre' McKitty (a third-round pick in 2021) and Brock Bowers, as well as Darnell Washington. – Seth Emerson

13 Connor Heyward
Michigan State (5-11, 239)

Heyward's Michigan State career was far from linear, but it all worked out in the end. Recruited as an athlete, Heyward was a jack-of-all-trades prospect who landed at running back at MSU. After being named the starter in 2019, Heyward lost his job and entered the transfer portal. But when Mel Tucker was hired in February 2020, Heyward chose to withdraw his name and finish his career at MSU. After a year in Jay Johnson's system, the new staff determined that Heyward — a natural receiver with some of the best hands on the team — had the skill set to thrive as a tight end/H-back. That decision paved the way for a strong senior season. – Colton Pouncy

14 Gerrit Prince
UAB (6-5, 240)

Prince was a touchdown maker for UAB. He caught a touchdown every 3.6 receptions. He averaged 19.4 yards per reception, and his 10 touchdowns was tied for third nationally for tight ends. He really showed what he could do against BYU in the 2021 Independence Bowl, when he caught two touchdowns passes in a 31-28 win over the Cougars. – Aaron Suttles

15 Grant Calcaterra
SMU (6-4, 236)

Calcaterra's career started at Oklahoma, and he was considered a top-50 draft prospect heading into the 2019 season, but concussion issues that year led him to voluntarily step away from football. He later decided to return to the game and enrolled at SMU in 2021, where he had a career-high 38 catches for 465 yards and four touchdowns. To protect himself, Calcaterra has extra padding in his helmet and wore a red uniform in practice. He remains the athletic talent he was at Oklahoma and had beefed up as a Mustang. – Chris Vannini

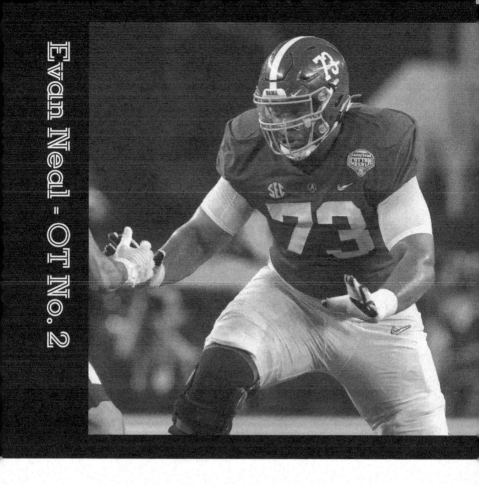

Offensive Tackles

1   Ikem Ekwonu
NC State (6-4, 322 pounds)

Even though he didn't make first-team all-ACC in 2020, Ekwonu was the O-lineman the coaches inside the conference were raving about last offseason. The quick-footed mauler cranked out pancakes by the dozens. A former high school wrestler who also ran the anchor leg on his high school track team, Ekwonu was overshadowed in the recruiting process by his twin brother Osita, now at Notre Dame, but the big man blossomed into a star in Raleigh, earning All-American honors in 2021 as the tone-setter for a top-20 team. – Bruce Feldman

2 Evan Neal
Alabama (6-7, 357)

On one of the most inconsistent offensive lines of the Nick Saban era, Evan Neal was the one sure thing the Alabama offense could count on. He's got prototypical size, but it's his athleticism at that size that has his draft stock so high. There's a video of the big man doing a box jump into the splits. He also showed versatility during his college career, starting at left guard, right tackle and left tackle. – Aaron Suttles

3 Charles Cross
Mississippi State (6-5, 305)

Few Bulldogs linemen were as prepared for the switch from coach Joe Moorhead to Mike Leach as Cross. He's lean with quick feet, and after playing only three games in Moorhead's final season in 2019, he became a starter as a redshirt freshman during Leach's first season in 2020. Playing alongside linemen recruited for run-heavy offenses favored by previous coaches Moorhead and Dan Mullen, Cross stood out because he was such an effective pass blocker for a team that averaged 50.6 pass attempts a game. But Cross was just as good moving forward as moving backward. SEC coaches named him first-team all-conference in 2021. – Andy Staples

4 Trevor Penning
Northern Iowa (6-7, 330)

For the second season in a row, Northern Iowa has built and developed a small-town Iowa offensive lineman into a high-round prospect. Penning follows Spencer Brown (now with the Bills) into the draft conversation after posting an even brighter resume. He was the only offensive lineman to be named as a finalist for the Walter Payton Award, which goes to the FCS player of the year. He appeared on eight All-America teams and helped lead the Panthers to a playoff appearance. – Scott Dochterman

5 Bernhard Raimann
Central Michigan (6-6, 304)

One of the most intriguing smaller-school prospects in the draft, Raimann brings an athletic frame and raw talent to a position he's only played for two seasons. He grew up in Austria, began playing football at age 14 and eventually moved to Michigan as part of a year-long foreign exchange program. After playing tight end for two seasons at Central Michigan, he gained 50 pounds and moved to left tackle prior to the pandemic-shortened 2020 season. He more than held his own in the Chippewas' games against LSU and Missouri early in the year, and he was named first-team all-MAC at the conclusion of the 2021 season. He's still a little lean, but he could play tackle or guard at the next level, and his speed, athleticism, agility and balance are all quite impressive. – Nicole Auerbach

6 Daniel Faalele
Minnesota (6-8, 387)

Faalele started eight games as a true freshman at Minnesota and never looked back, making 31 starts at right tackle in all and anchoring one of the Big Ten's top offensive lines, a unit that paved the way for a strong rushing attack despite multiple serious injuries to running backs in recent years. The hulking native of Melbourne, Australia, was named first-team All-Big Ten by the league's coaches in 2021 and was honorable mention all-conference in 2018 and 2019. – Matt Fortuna

7 Max Mitchell
Louisiana (6-6, 299)

One thing Billy Napier's Louisiana staffs always did well was develop offensive linemen, and Mitchell is a versatile prospect who played both tackle spots when needed. After being All-Sun Belt in 2020, he earned national acclaim as a consensus All-American in 2021. Pro Football Focus named him a first-team All-American with the highest PFF grade (95.1) of any lineman in the country last fall. – Brody Miller

8 Tyler Smith
Tulsa (6-5, 332)

Smith used his massive frame well while at Tulsa. After seeing limited action in 2019 as a redshirt, Smith broke out in 2020, starting all nine games at left tackle en route to earning All-America and all-conference honors. In 2021 he got even better, becoming one of the nation's best run blockers: His 93.9 run block grade from Pro Football Focus was fourth-best in the FBS. He proved a solid pass protector as well, allowing just two sacks in 446 pass-blocking snaps. – Sam Kahn Jr.

9 Abraham Lucas
Washington State (6-6, 322)

A four-year starter at right tackle, Lucas earned first-team All-Pac-12 honors in 2021 to cap a career that included 42 consecutive starts and began with Freshman All-America recognition. He finished 2021 with the best pass protection grade in the conference, per PFF. He also had the top run-blocking grade on the team, and the top offensive grade overall. – Christian Caple

10 Nicholas Petit-Frere
Ohio State (6-5, 304)

Petit-Frere was one of the top tackle prospects in the 2018 recruiting class, but it took him a couple of years to lock down a starting job, which he did on a full-time basis entering the 2020 season. All told, he started 20 games at left tackle for the Buckeyes, performing at a first-team all-conference level as a senior in 2021. He was a reliable pass protector on the blind side for both Justin Fields and C.J. Stroud, and one of the more athletic linemen to come through the program in the last 10 years. – Bill Landis

11 Rasheed Walker
Penn State (6-6, 320)

Walker saw the field early at Penn State, appearing in four games in 2018 as a true freshman. Over the next three seasons he started 32 consecutive games at left tackle before missing the final three games of his career with an undisclosed injury. A 2021 team captain and a player whose frame has long made him appealing to college and NFL suitors, Walker's production was up and down. Penn State's entire line struggled last season, as no back rushed for 100 yards in a game. Walker was a third-team All-Big Ten honoree by the conference's coaches in 2021. – Audrey Snyder

12 Spencer Burford
UTSA (6-4, 293)

From the time he arrived in San Antonio, Burford was reliable and consistent. The four-year starter spent his first two seasons at guard before shifting to tackle in his last two seasons. In 2020-21, Burford anchored a unit that paved the way for one of the nation's most productive running backs, Sincere McCormick, who rushed for nearly 3,000 combined yards in the last two seasons. A 2021 first-team All-Conference USA pick, Burford allowed only two sacks in 420 pass-blocking snaps according to Pro Football Focus. Primarily a left tackle, Burford proved versatile enough to play either side. – Sam Kahn Jr.

13 Braxton Jones
Southern Utah (6-5, 306)

A two-star prospect in high school, Jones attracted minimal recruiting interest. Yet at Southern Utah, he became a star left tackle and NFL prospect. As a sophomore, Jones earned FCS All-America recognition, drawing the attention of pro scouts. Last season he anchored a line that gave up 1.82 sacks per game. Jones finished as a two-time All-Big Sky selection and as an all-academic honoree. – Doug Haller

14 Dare Rosenthal
Kentucky (6-7, 305)

The culture of UK's offensive line room was the perfect rehab for Rosenthal's image after running into some trouble at LSU, where he started eight games in two seasons, including three starts for the 2019 national championship team. The massive former four-star recruit lived up to his promise in a full-time starting role for the Wildcats at left tackle. He was so steady and athletic there that it allowed potential first-round pick Darian Kinnard to stay at right tackle. In a dozen starts for UK, Rosenthal allowed just one sack after giving up only two sacks in as many seasons at LSU. – Kyle Tucker

15 Kellen Diesch
Arizona State (6-7, 292)

Diesch played in 21 games over three seasons at Texas A&M, yet he never started once. A 2020 transfer to Arizona State changed his college career. In Tempe, Diesch pretty much was locked in at left tackle from Day 1. Not long into his first season, offensive coordinator Zak Hill said Diesch, who played defensive end and tight end for most of his high school career, looked like a pro prospect. This past season, Diesch was an All-Pac-12 second team selection. – Doug Haller

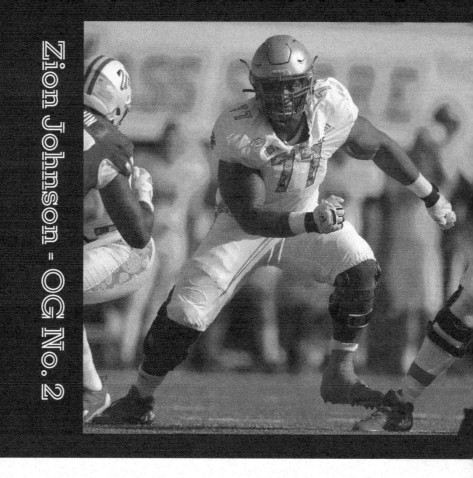

Guards

1 Kenyon Green
Texas A&M (6-4, 325 pounds)

The former five-star recruit was a Day 1 starter and never missed a game. He made the SEC All-Freshman team as a right guard in 2019, was a first-team All-American at left guard in 2020 and showed his versatility in his final season on campus. In 2021, Green was the only FBS player to log at least 80 snaps at four different offensive line positions. He played all five positions in his career but did his best work as a run blocker at guard. Green gave A&M a dependable, consistent leader up front. – Sam Kahn Jr.

2 Zion Johnson
Boston College (6-3, 314)

Johnson received All-America honors from seven different organizations in 2021. The left guard was first-team All-ACC this past season, the third time that he made one of the league's all-conference teams. ESPN's advanced stats say he did not allow a single pressure in 2021. He allowed just one sack in his entire Boston College career. The 6-foot-3, 316-pound native of Bowie, Md., had started 19 games at Davidson before transferring to BC ahead of the 2019 season, when he made an immediate impact. – Matt Fortuna

3 Darian Kinnard
Kentucky (6-5, 324)

He came back for his senior season to solidify his NFL Draft status, and to that end, it's hard to do more than he did. Kinnard won the Jacobs Blocking Trophy as the SEC's top lineman and became just the 12th consensus All-American in school history. He led Kentucky's "Big Blue Wall," finalists for the Joe Moore Award, with 30 knockdown blocks. He was one of just three Power 5 tackles who graded 85 percent or better as both run and pass blockers, per Pro Football Focus. Kinnard was the picture of reliability with 39 consecutive starts and so few penalties and sacks allowed in four years that you could count them each on one hand. – Kyle Tucker

4 Jamaree Salyer
Georgia (6-3, 320)

Salyer came to Georgia as a five-star recruit and lived up to it. He was a three-year starter and leader, and a versatile one: He was the starting left tackle for the better part of his career but also played guard, which many assumed would be his future NFL position. At left tackle, Salyer went against the likes of Aidan Hutchinson and Will Anderson and did very well. Salyer was also a backup center, showing his range of talent and ability. – Seth Emerson

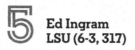 **Ed Ingram**
LSU (6-3, 317)

Often described as LSU's most talented offensive lineman while in Baton Rouge, Ingram became a key piece with 34 career starts at multiple positions during a difficult time for LSU up front. He was a rotational piece during LSU's national title run in 2019 before having up-and-down results the past two seasons. Still, he was a clear leader for LSU and an athletic and versatile piece. – Brody Miller

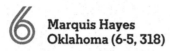 **Marquis Hayes**
Oklahoma (6-5, 318)

Hayes started 37 games at left guard over the last three seasons for Oklahoma, becoming a mainstay on the Sooners' offensive line. Throughout those years, the Sooners rushed for 7,766 yards and 94 touchdowns, averaging 5.42 yards per rush over that stretch. Hayes allowed five sacks during his time as a starter, according to Pro Football Focus data. The Sooners have had six offensive linemen drafted since 2018. – Jason Kersey

7 **Lecitus Smith**
Virginia Tech (6-3, 321)

The one-time blocking tight end coming out of high school grew into an offensive lineman pretty quickly and was a mainstay up front for the Hokies, starting 38 games over his final four seasons and earning an All-ACC honorable mention three times. He's got good size and is a powerful, physical blocker, having played his whole career almost exclusively at left guard. – Andy Bitter

Luke Goedeke
Central Michigan (6-5, 310)

Goedeke is the lesser-known Chippewas tackle next to Bernhard Raimann, but scouts who checked in on Central Michigan got to see two small-school studs on the same offensive line. Goedeke, a 2021 first-team All-MAC selection, missed most of his senior year of high school due to a shoulder injury and began his collegiate career at Division III Wisconsin-Stevens Point as a tight end. He started all 14 games for the Chippewas in 2019 and missed the 2020 season due to a knee injury. This past season, as the right tackle bookending the line with Raimann, Goedeke helped CMU to a 9-4 record (including the MAC's first-ever win over a Pac-12 opponent in the Sun Bowl) and helped pave the way for running back Lew Nichols III to become the nation's leading rusher. – Nicole Auerbach

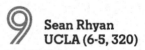

Sean Rhyan
UCLA (6-5, 320)

The most highly touted recruit in UCLA's 2019 class, Rhyan was a big get for Chip Kelly, who loved his combination of size and agility. Rhyan also excelled in track, throwing the shot put and the discus. He became the first freshman to start a season opener at offensive tackle in seven years for the Bruins and proceeded to start every game of his college career in three seasons, becoming a driving force in the nation's No. 17 rushing attack in 2021 and making the Pac-12 coaches' first-team all-league honors. – Bruce Feldman

10 Chris Paul
Tulsa (6-3, 324)

Paul was a four-year starter at Tulsa who played all over the line. He started one season at right guard, one at left guard, one at right tackle and began 2021 at left tackle before moving back to the right side. He earned all-conference honors twice and earned other honors and respect for his work off the field. Paul was a student-athlete representative on the NCAA's football oversight committee, he was on several other student-athlete committees, and he has released two songs, holding a live performance in November. – Chris Vannini

11 Thayer Munford
Ohio State (6-6, 327)

Former offensive line coach Greg Studrawa had to lobby Urban Meyer to take Munford, a four-star in-state product, as a late addition in the 2017 recruiting class. Munford ended up being a stalwart on the offensive line. He started 33 games over three seasons at left tackle before switching to left guard and starting 12 games there in 2021. He earned first-team all-conference honors at both tackle and guard, establishing himself as one of the best offensive linemen in the Big Ten over the last two seasons. – Bill Landis

12 Joshua Ezeudu
North Carolina (6-4, 325)

A three-year starter at North Carolina, Ezeudu has experience at guard and tackle, although he was an interior player last season for the Tar Heels. While North Carolina was a disappointment last season, Ezeudu helped the Tar Heels finish No. 18 nationally in yards per carry. He was also starting on an offensive line that finished dead last among Power 5 programs in sacks allowed with 49 on the season. Only Liberty and Akron were worse nationally. Ezeudu's inside-out versatility could be an asset at the next level. – Pete Sampson

13 Andrew Stueber
Michigan (6-6, 327)

Stueber overcame a knee injury in 2019 to have a standout career at Michigan, capped by his performance at right tackle for an offensive line that won the Joe Moore Award in 2021. His ability to play guard or tackle made him a player who always found his way onto the field, regardless of the other talent surrounding him. Stueber started 22 games at Michigan, the majority of those at right tackle, but he may profile best as a guard in the NFL. Either way, he has the size, the experience and the football IQ to be an asset. – Austin Meek

14 Justin Shaffer
Georgia (6-4, 326)

Shaffer was the perfect example of development: A three-star prospect, he saw a little playing time as a freshman, a bit more as a sophomore, then started six games as a junior and became a starter as a senior. Shaffer took advantage of the COVID-19 extra year and returned for the 2021 season, starting every game and playing both guard spots. He may not come off as a huge prospect, but his steady improvement every year in college could continue into the pros. – Seth Emerson

15 Cade Mays
Tennessee (6-5, 321)

Mays' two biggest assets are his versatility and his size. At Georgia, he played every position on the line but center and was slated to start at left tackle before transferring home to Tennessee. He spent time at guard and tackle before finding a home at right tackle. He's a mauler in the run game and has a ton of experience as a four-year starter in the SEC who entered the league as a five-star recruit. – David Ubben

Centers

1 Tyler Linderbaum
Iowa (6-3, 292 pounds)

The best center in Kirk Ferentz's Iowa tenure, Linderbaum switched from defensive tackle following the 2018 season and earned the starting role by spring 2019. He was Pro Football Focus' highest-graded center in 2020 and 2021, became the 10th unanimous All-American in Iowa history following the 2021 season and won the Rimington Trophy. Linderbaum, a Dean's List student who graduated in less than four years, combines elite balance, power, quickness and explosiveness with tenacity and a rare competitive streak. For some teams, he's undersized. But few, if any, centers can reach and bury a three-technique like Linderbaum. – Scott Dochterman

2 Dylan Parham
Memphis (6-2, 313)

Parham was an ironman for Memphis, starting all 51 Tigers games over the past four seasons. He came to Memphis as a tight end and redshirted his first season, but he moved to offensive line heading into the 2018 season and immediately became a starter. He earned first-team All-AAC honors as a senior in 2021. He spent this past year as the right guard but has also started at left guard and right tackle, so he can move around the line. – Chris Vannini

3 Cole Strange
Chattanooga (6-4, 304)

Strange was a Freshman All-American and a three-time All-Southern Conference talent with the Mocs, finding a home at left guard throughout his career. He has great speed and was used often as a puller in the offense. He was a force in the run game and was twice given the Jacobs Blocking Trophy as the conference's best offensive lineman. – David Ubben

4 Dohnovan West
Arizona State (6-3, 315)

A three-star prospect out of California, West made an immediate impact in college, starting all 13 games as a true freshman: the first two at center, the rest at right guard. In 2020, West started at left guard and became an All-Pac-12 selection. Ahead of his third season, Arizona State shifted West to center because the staff thought it was the position he would play at the next level. West again excelled, anchoring the line and earning All-Pac-12 second-team recognition. – Doug Haller

5 Cam Jurgens
Nebraska (6-3, 290)

Jurgens dealt the Huskers a blow by leaving two years of collegiate eligibility on the table after starting for three consecutive seasons. His strong run at center followed a redshirt season and a switch from tight end, the position at which he was recruited in 2018 out of Beatrice, Neb., by the likes of LSU. A freakish athlete, Jurgens brought explosive play and an aggressive mentality in anchoring the Huskers up front with 18 consecutive games to complete his time in Lincoln. He struggled early in his career with a foot injury and snapping inconsistency, but he has apparently put all of it behind him. – Mitch Sherman

6 Luke Fortner
Kentucky (6-4, 302)

Fortner started 36 consecutive games for the Wildcats' bruising O-line, taking advantage of the free COVID-19 year for a sixth season in Lexington and teaming up with Dare Rosenthal and Darian Kinnard to solidify a unit that was a finalist for the Joe Moore Award in 2021. On top of his leadership bona fides on the field, he was also inducted into the Frank G. Ham Society of Character, which recognizes Wildcat student-athletes who excel in academic, athletic and personal development endeavors. – Eric Single

7 Alec Lindstrom
Boston College (6-3, 302)

A two-time, first-team ACC center, Lindstrom started 36 games the past three seasons. He's the younger brother of former Boston College guard Chris Lindstrom, a former first-round pick of the Atlanta Falcons. The younger Lindstrom allowed just one sack all last season, even though the Eagles allowed 24 as a team. Judging his fifth year at Chestnut Hill is a challenge because starting quarterback Phil Jurkovec missed most of the season with a hand injury that never fully healed. – Pete Sampson

8 Dawson Deaton
Texas Tech (6-5, 300)

After a freshman season where the versatile offensive lineman served as a rotational player and spot starter, Deaton quickly found his home at center and never budged. He appeared in 45 of 47 possible games in his four-year Texas Tech career, starting as the full-time center for the last three. Deaton earned second-team All-Big 12 honors in 2020 and 2021 and shined as a senior, allowing only one sack on 378 pass-blocking snaps, per PFF. He was also a team captain who played in multiple schemes. – Sam Khan Jr.

9 James Empey
BYU (6-4, 289)

Empey, the son of a former BYU captain, took a circuitous route to Provo after starring at American Fork (Utah) High School. He originally signed with Utah but delayed his enrollment for a mission in Portugal. Upon his return, Empey opted to play for rival BYU, where his father Mike was the Cougars' offensive line coach at the time. Empey ended up starting 13 games in both his redshirt freshman and sophomore seasons but was slowed by injury in both 2020 and 2021. He missed the final six games this past fall with a lower-body injury. He ended his career at BYU with 41 games played and 41 starts. – Mitch Light

10 Nick Ford
Utah (6-5, 315)

A lightly recruited three-star prospect from San Pedro, Calif., Ford emerged as one of the top offensive linemen in the nation during his time at Utah. He made starts at all five positions on the line but spent most of his time on the interior, with 24 starts at guard and 15 at center. He earned first-team All-Pac 12 honors in both 2020 and 2021 and was an honorable mention pick in 2019. – Mitch Light

11 Luke Wattenberg
Washington (6-5, 297)

When Wattenberg stepped in for an injured Trey Adams at left tackle in 2017, it began a streak of 48 consecutive starts: five at left tackle, 27 at left guard and 16 the past two seasons at center as he exercised his sixth year of eligibility. Coaches moved him to center to take advantage of his experience and IQ, and Wattenberg became a key offensive leader. He didn't quite develop into the all-conference lineman some may have envisioned when he became the rare four-star prospect from Southern California to sign with UW despite offers from both USC and UCLA, but Wattenberg nevertheless turned in a solid career and would bring a wealth of experience to an NFL roster. – Christian Caple

12 Doug Kramer
Illinois (6-2, 306)

Kramer took advantage of the free COVID-19 year of eligibility to return to Illinois in 2021. A three-time team captain, Kramer started all 48 games in which he played during his five active seasons (he redshirted in 2016). He earned second-team All-Big Ten honors in 2021 and was an honorable mention pick in both 2019 and 2020. The Hinsdale, Ill., native was lightly recruited coming out of high school and didn't receive an offer from Illinois — where both of his parents went to school — until very late in the process. – Mitch Light

Edge Rushers

1 Aidan Hutchinson
Michigan (6-6, 261)

Hutchinson's decision to bypass the 2021 draft couldn't have worked out much better. As a senior, he led Michigan to a Big Ten championship, finished second in the Heisman Trophy voting and put himself in contention to be the No. 1 pick. Moving from defensive end to stand-up edge rusher, Hutchinson finished third in the FBS with 14 sacks in 2021 after recording 4.5 in his first three years at Michigan. He is known as a high-motor player, but he's also a freaky athlete. – Austin Meek

2 Kayvon Thibodeaux
Oregon (6-4, 255)

The No. 1 recruit in the country three years ago, Thibodeaux was tested daily at practice as a freshman going up against powerhouse Oregon offensive lineman Penei Sewell. Thibodeaux could be dominant at times: In 31 career games, he had 19 sacks and 34.5 tackles for loss. Against UCLA this season, he had nine tackles and two sacks in a big road win. In three Pac-12 title games, he had 21 quarterback pressures, 5.5 TFLs and 4.5 sacks. He battled injuries in 2021 and was sidelined with an ankle injury for the Ducks' big win at Ohio State. – Bruce Feldman

3 Travon Walker
Georgia (6-5, 275)

Walker was blocked from a starting spot at defensive end his first two years, but his talent was still evident to the coaches. Once the way was cleared Walker's junior year, he was dominant. He could rush the passer, help the dominant run defense and even drop into coverage. As physically imposing as he is, Walker's athletic ability was also evident on a handful of plays when he ran to make open-field tackles. – Seth Emerson

4 David Ojabo
Michigan (6-5, 275)

It would be hard to find a prospect who enhanced his stock more than Ojabo did in 2021. Ojabo entered the season with fewer than 30 career snaps but emerged as one of the top pass rushers in college football with 11 sacks and five forced fumbles. He has room to grow but is more than just a raw athlete, as his repertoire of pass rush moves demonstrates. Ojabo will need to improve as a run defender to be an every-down player in the NFL, but he was dynamic for Michigan as a pass rush specialist in 2021. – Austin Meek

5 Jermaine Johnson
Florida State (6-4, 259)

Johnson took a winding path to becoming the 2021 ACC Defensive Player of the Year. The Eden Prairie, Minn., will likely be the highest draft pick to appear on the Netflix series Last Chance U. He played at Independence (Kan.) Junior College in 2017 and 2018 before transferring to Georgia. Johnson had five sacks and 11 QB pressures for the Bulldogs in 2020 and would have played a big role on the 2021 Georgia defense that helped the Bulldogs win the national title, but Johnson wanted to prove he could be an every-down player. He did that at Florida State, where he was the best player on the roster the moment he stepped on campus. In 2021, Johnson made 70 tackles with 18 for loss. Twelve of those were sacks. He also proved stout setting the edge against the run. – Andy Staples

6 George Karlaftis
Purdue (6-4, 268)

Karlaftis was named an AFCA first-team All-American in 2021 and a first-team All-Big Ten defensive end, in addition to being a semifinalist or finalist for multiple national defensive player awards. The ballyhooed prospect who was born in Athens, Greece, before moving to West Lafayette, Ind., finished his college career with 25.5 tackles for loss across three seasons, with 12.5 sacks, one interception, five passes defended, four forced fumbles, two fumble recoveries and one blocked kick. – Matt Fortuna

7 Logan Hall
Houston (6-6, 278)

The Cougars were loaded on the defensive line, but Hall was the best of the bunch. The big, physical, relentless defensive lineman produced both off the edge and on the interior, finishing with 13 tackles for loss and six sacks en route to first-team all-conference honors in 2021. Hall's quickness helped him shine as a pass rusher and as a run defender. Coaches loved his intensity, noting he played the same way every play in practice as he did on Saturdays. Off the field, he was a great teammate with a quiet demeanor. – Sam Khan Jr.

8 Arnold Ebiketie
Penn State (6-2, 250)

Temple knew it had a playmaker, and Penn State reaped the rewards. Ebiketie became a starter after arriving in Happy Valley as a grad transfer and made an instant impact for his final season. The most disruptive player on Penn State's defensive line, Ebiketie started 12 games and finished with 9.5 sacks, 18 TFLs and two forced fumbles. He also blocked a pair of field goals. It's quite the journey for the player who grew up playing soccer in Cameroon. Ebiketie started playing football in the states in 10th grade and transformed from a high school wide receiver and linebacker to a collegiate defensive end. – Audrey Snyder

9 Drake Jackson
USC (6-4, 255)

The Trojans won a hard-fought recruiting battle with Arizona State to land Jackson, who paid immediate dividends as a freshman with 5.5 sacks and 11.5 tackles for loss. Jackson flashed a high ceiling that year but never quite captured the same consistency over his final two seasons and played at a much lower weight than the 275 pounds he played at his freshman year. USC utilized him in coverage at times, but he's best suited as a pass rusher who could make some plays against the run with his athleticism. – Antonio Morales

10 Kingsley Enagbare
South Carolina (6-4, 261)

Enagbare was a backup for his first two seasons before breaking out as a junior in 2020 in the pandemic-shortened season. Enagbare excelled in the Buck (rush LB) position in former Gamecocks coach Will Muschamp's defense. In eight games that season, Enagbare had six sacks and three forced fumbles. As a senior playing for Shane Beamer in 2021, Enagbare was named South Carolina's defensive MVP after leading the Gamecocks in tackles for loss (7.5) and sacks (4). – Andy Staples

11 Myjai Sanders
Cincinnati (6-4, 242)

A true edge rusher whose numbers took a dip in 2021 as opposing offenses double-teamed and schemed against him, finishing with just 2.5 sacks and 7.5 tackles for loss. But he added 13 quarterback hits and six pass breakups at the line of scrimmage, and he has always been underrated as a run stopper. He needs to put weight on his frame, which was a struggle at Cincinnati, but his quick first step and relentless motor should benefit him at the next level. – Justin Williams

12 Alex Wright
UAB (6-7, 270)

The 6-7, 270-pound junior started 18 games over his three-year college career, including eight in 2021 when he earned second-team All-Conference USA honors. He finished with 46 tackles, 7.5 for loss, with seven sacks, three pass breakups, two forced fumbles and 51 pressures created on 276 pass rushing snaps according to Pro Football Focus. Over his career at UAB, Wright produced 19 tackles for loss and 11.5 sacks to go with 91 tackles. – Manny Navarro

13 Boye Mafe
Minnesota (6-4, 255)

With National team MVP honors at the Senior Bowl, Mafe displayed the same type of skill set in front of pro scouts that he showed opposing Big Ten offenses for four years. Mafe's violent hands and explosive first step made him a powerful pass rusher for the Gophers from both three-point and stand-up positions. He finished with 15 sacks (ninth in Minnesota history) and 19.5 tackles for loss in 42 games. Last fall, Mafe earned second-team All-Big Ten honors. – Scott Dochterman

14 Dominique Robinson
Miami-Ohio (6-5, 254)

For three seasons, Robinson played as an oversized wide receiver at Miami (Ohio) and started 13 games in 2018-19. Then in the shortened 2020 season, Robinson switched to defensive line and made an immediate impression with two sacks in his first of three games. Last fall, Robinson picked up 4.5 sacks and four quarterback hurries. With long arms and raw athletic ability, Robinson has the potential to become an impact player with time. – Scott Dochterman

15 DeAngelo Malone
Western Kentucky (6-3, 234)

A two-time Conference USA Defensive Player of the Year, Malone was a force for most of his five-year college career, finishing with a school record 34 sacks. As a senior, Malone posted 94 tackles, which led all FBS defensive linemen. He also had 17.5 tackles for loss and nine sacks. At the 2022 Senior Bowl, Malone was named the American Team's MVP after collecting six tackles and two quarterback hurries. – Doug Haller

Defensive Tackles

1 Devonte Wyatt
Georgia (6-3, 307)

A three-year starter, Wyatt emerged as a force in his final season. Prior to that he had been overshadowed by Jordan Davis and others on the defensive line, but as a senior Wyatt tallied seven tackles for loss and 39 tackles. Wyatt was the classic case of gradual improvement, starting as a three-star prospect (by Rivals and ESPN) who needed one semester in junior college to academically qualify, then playing as a reserve his freshman season at Georgia. He played mostly tackle for the Bulldogs, with some snaps at end and nose. – **Seth Emerson**

2 Jordan Davis
Georgia (6-6, 360)

Only a three-star prospect coming out of Charlotte, N.C., Davis showed immediately that he was underrated, forcing his way into the lineup midway through his freshman year and staying there the rest of his college career. His impact went well beyond the stat sheet (three career sacks, 11.5 TFL) as Davis swallowed up blockers and was a big reason Georgia's run base was dominant the past three seasons. He also pushed the pocket enough to help teammates get to the quarterback. For his efforts, Kirby Smart rewarded him with a rushing touchdown during his senior year. – **Seth Emerson**

3 Travis Jones
Connecticut (6-4, 326)

Jones didn't have a 2020 season, as UConn was one of two FBS teams to opt out due to COVID-19 concerns. But he had a solid 2021, finishing with 48 tackles, 7.5 tackles for loss and 4.5 sacks from the defensive tackle position, and he racked up eight sacks over his final two seasons. He's got the size and awareness on the field, and Jones was also part of the team's leadership council. – **Chris Vannini**

4 DeMarvin Leal
Texas A&M (6-4, 290)

Leal was a versatile, impactful defensive lineman at A&M. His size, strength and athleticism made him a force both on the interior and off the edge. The three-year starter led Aggies with 12.5 tackles for loss and 8.5 sacks en route to All-America and first-team All-SEC honors in 2021. Leal's flexibility allowed A&M to be creative in deploying personnel on its defensive front and he proved disruptive wherever the Aggies lined him up, regardless of the caliber of his opponent. He could have been more consistent, but overall he lived up to his five-star recruit status in Aggieland. – **Sam Khan Jr.**

5 Perrion Winfrey
Oklahoma (6-4, 303)

At his best, Winfrey was arguably the most dominant Oklahoma interior defensive lineman since Gerald McCoy, a first-round pick in 2010 and six-time Pro Bowler. He wasn't the most consistent player, but his flashes showed what kind of talent he has and what kind of NFL player he could become. A transfer from Iowa Western Community College, Winfrey was an immediate starter at OU and finished his two-year Sooners career with six sacks and 16.5 TFLs.
– Jason Kersey

6 Phidarian Mathis
Alabama (6-4, 318)

Mathis lived up to the offseason buzz in 2021 and became a solid player on the defensive line. He was second on the team in sacks (9) and third in tackles for loss (10.5). He has maximized his ability, and it showed in his senior season with the Crimson Tide. He had his best game against LSU with nine tackles, including seven solo, and 1.5 tackles for loss. – Aaron Suttles

7 John Ridgeway
Arkansas (6-5, 327)

After a standout career at Illinois State, Ridgeway graduated and transferred for one season at Arkansas. He made four tackles for loss, two sacks and 39 tackles. His 6-foot-6, 320-pound frame is imposing as an interior lineman. He's strong and has good lateral quickness and handled consistent double teams well last season as a nose guard in Arkansas' 3-2-6 scheme. He was a major asset for the Razorbacks' run defense. – David Ubben

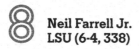

Neil Farrell Jr.
LSU (6-4, 338)

One of the unsung heroes of LSU's 2019 title defense, Farrell finally broke out as one of the top interior linemen in the SEC this fall with 9.5 tackles for loss and 13 run stuffs, per Sports Info Solutions. As LSU's defense grew depleted by injuries and opt-outs in 2021, Farrell was the anchor of a run defense that suddenly ranked top three in the SEC the final five weeks. Even coming off the bench in 2019, he led LSU linemen with 46 tackles and seven for loss. He's athletic and disruptive in the middle. – Brody Miller

Kalia Davis
UCF (6-2, 310)

The 2017 former three-star linebacker recruit from Pensacola, Fla., played and started in only five games over his final two college seasons after sitting out the 2020 season because of COVID-19 and suffering a season-ending knee injury in October last season. He was effective, though, grading out well according to Pro Football Focus in 2019 and 2021 when he produced 44 tackles, 12.5 for loss, with four sacks over a 16-game stretch that featured 14 starts. – Manny Navarro

Eyioma Uwazurike
Iowa State (6-6, 310)

Uwazurike trusted he could take his game to another level if he took advantage of his extra season of eligibility in 2021. The super senior became one of the Big 12's best defensive linemen, finishing No. 4 in the conference in sacks and pressures and earning first-team All-Big 12 honors. During his six years in Ames, Uwazurike played in 60 games with 46 starts, provided impressive leadership and proved versatile enough to make an impact as both an interior lineman and edge defender. – Scott Dochterman

11   Otito Ogbonnia
UCLA (6-4, 326)

UCLA had a solid run defense in 2021, and Ogbonnia played a critical role in that. Ogbonnia started all 12 games as an imposing presence along the interior of the Bruins' defensive front. He finished with 30 total tackles, five for loss, two sacks and a forced fumble in 2021, which was his lone season as a starter. Ogbonnia also has a track and field background in the shot put; he placed 10th in the NCAA championships during the 2018-19 season. – Antonio Morales

12   Haskell Garrett
Ohio State (6-1, 298)

Garrett played at an All-America level alongside Tommy Togiai in 2020, forming one of the better tackle duos in the country and helping Ohio State reach the national championship that season. He somewhat surprisingly came back for a fifth season in 2021 and didn't quite match that level of play. Still, he was a steady and reliable interior pass rusher for two years, and a captain in his final season. – Bill Landis

13   Noah Elliss
Idaho (6-4, 360)

Elliss is the son of Luther Elliss, a former NFL defensive lineman who made two Pro Bowls over a 10-year career and is now the defensive line coach at Idaho. A three-star high school prospect, Elliss originally signed with Mississippi State before ending up at Idaho. With the Vandals, he played in 21 games, totaling 93 tackles, 10 for loss and three quarterback sacks. Older brothers Kaden (31 games) and Christian (1) also have played in the NFL. – Doug Haller

14 Marquan McCall
Kentucky (6-3, 358)

You don't earn the nickname "Bully Ball McCall" unless you can push people around. McCall is like a lot of nose guards: much more impactful than his stats. The 57 tackles, 10 for loss, in 40 career games hardly tell the tale. McCall took on double teams and cleared the way for a talented group of linebackers to clean up after him. Kentucky ranked 20th nationally in run defense last season, with lots of help from McCall. "Marquan can really dictate a game, not necessarily by stats but by what he forces an offense to do," UK defensive coordinator Brad White said. "He'll make life easier for other guys." – **Kyle Tucker**

15 Thomas Booker
Stanford (6-4, 310)

A former national prospect who chose Stanford over Notre Dame, Booker started games in each of his four seasons with the Cardinal and was a two-time captain. Recruited as a jumbo defensive end out of high school, Booker grew into an athletic interior defensive lineman in Palo Alto. While Booker never quite hit the heights of his national recruiting profile, he finished with 20.5 TFLs and 9.5 sacks in 41 career games as the Cardinal defense struggled for much of the defensive lineman's college career. – **Pete Sampson**

Devin Lloyd - LB No. 1

Linebackers

1   Devin Lloyd
Utah (6-3, 232)

Utah has long been known as a factory for NFL defensive prospects, but it wasn't until Lloyd's emergence that the Utes truly showcased what a versatile, all-around linebacker could do behind their talented defensive line. Lloyd's size allowed him to be a jack-of-all-trades either as a blitzing linebacker, in coverage against a tight end or at times coming off the edge to provide extra pressure. If Lloyd goes to a team with an up-and-coming defensive corps, he'll be able to slide in and fill a similar role as the quarterback of a defense just like he was at Utah. – **Christopher Kamrani**

2 Nakobe Dean
Georgia (6-0, 225)

Dean arrived a year after the departure of Roquan Smith and was frequently compared to him, and his career followed the same trajectory: a reserve as a freshman, followed by two years as the starter and unofficial captain of the front defense, perhaps the entire defense. Dean led Georgia in tackles as a sophomore and led the team in tackles for loss as a junior, including six sacks, showing his blend of playmaking and consistency. Off the field, he was also an excellent student. – Seth Emerson

3 Quay Walker
Georgia (6-4, 245)

Walker was yet another highly-ranked recruit who had to wait his turn for major playing time at Georgia, only to see it pay off in a huge way. Walker was a top-50 recruit who didn't start a game (even then only two) until his junior year, but he became the starter in 2021 and ended up third on the team in tackles. Every year his snaps went up, along with his tackles: From six as a freshman to 23 then 43 and finally 67. – Seth Emerson

4 Chad Muma
Wyoming (6-2, 236)

Muma was a tackling machine at Wyoming, and his 142 tackles in 2021 were one away from the most in the nation. He reached at least nine tackles in 12 of 13 games last season, and he finished No. 3 nationally in tackles-per-game in 2020 after earning a starting position. Muma also grabbed three interceptions in 2021, returning two for touchdowns. He arrived at Wyoming as a safety/linebacker, before settling into the linebacker role, but that background is evident in his ability to play zone coverage. – Chris Vannini

5 Christian Harris
Alabama (6-2, 232)

Harris brings a ton of athleticism and quick twitch at inside linebacker. He started on the Alabama defense as a freshman, which speaks to his ability to adjust quickly. He compiled 79 tackles in 2021, and his 12.5 tackles for loss was second on the team. He also has experience in calling the defense, which he did his first two seasons. – Aaron Suttles

6 Leo Chenal
Wisconsin (6-2, 252)

Chenal is a weight-room warrior whose physicality stands out on the field. He led Wisconsin last year in tackles (115) and tackles for loss (18.5) while finishing second in sacks (eight) despite missing the first two games of his junior season due to COVID-19. According to Pro Football Focus, he ranked first among linebackers in run defense grade (94.1) and second in pass rush grade (91.8). Chenal's intensity, explosiveness and ability to blow up a play should translate well to the NFL, although he needs to improve his pass coverage skills. – Jesse Temple

7 Brian Asamoah
Oklahoma (6-0, 222)

Asamoah entered the starting lineup in 2020, his third season on campus, and quickly became one of the Sooners' most productive defenders. He led OU in tackles in each of the last two seasons, finishing his career with 179 tackles, 13 TFLs, five sacks, three forced fumbles and an interception. A 2021 Butkus Award semifinalist, Asamoah at his best was one of the better linebackers in the BIg 12 Conference and has been praised for his freakish athletic ability. – Jason Kersey

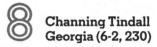

Channing Tindall
Georgia (6-2, 230)

Tindall could be one of the best Georgia players to never actually a start a game: He was almost always in the two-deep – as a freshman he had a sack in the 2018 SEC championship – but was never the starter, stuck behind Nakobe Dean, Monty Rice and his senior year in a rotation with classmate Quay Walker. But Tindall still played enough to rack up 12 career sacks, including 5.5 as a senior, when he was also fourth on the team in tackles. – Seth Emerson

Troy Andersen
Montana State (6-3, 242)

Andersen holds the unique accolades of being named Big Sky freshman of the year at running back (2017), first-team All-Big Sky at quarterback (2018) and national defensive player of the year at linebacker (2021) across three different seasons. He can play — and play well – all over the field. He finished with 150 tackles in 2021 and was named to the national all-scholar team. Not many linebackers hold school rushing records, but Andersen is one of the most intriguing players in the draft because of his versatility. – Chris Vannini

Damone Clark
LSU (6-2, 245)

Few players carried as much potential at LSU as Clark, and he finally made good on that potential in 2021. After a troubled 2020 season in which he got benched, Clark evolved into a Butkus Award finalist this year with 137 tackles and 15.5 tackles for loss, gliding sideline to sideline on a unit that ended the year playing elite SEC defense. He also spent two years as LSU's No. 18, the number given to a high-character leader. Clark is still just scratching the surface of his ability, and he's already a star. – Brody Miller

11 JoJo Domann
Nebraska (6-1, 229)

No one did more defensively for Nebraska over the past two seasons. The Huskers basically created a position for Domann, who rarely came off the field in playing a hybrid safety-outside linebacker spot that allowed the Huskers to match various looks with minimal substitutions. He defends well in space against speed and size at tight end and can hold his own against wideouts while playing with the physicality to cut down running backs at the point of attack. A thumb injury ended his sixth season with the Huskers before the final two games, but he still earned second-team All-America recognition from the Associated Press and Pro Football Focus. – Mitch Sherman

12 Terrel Bernard
Baylor (6-1, 220)

When healthy, Bernard served as a tackling machine for the Bears. He burst onto the scene as a sophomore, racking up 112 stops to finish second in the Big 12. His junior season was cut short by a knee injury, but he closed out his career in stellar fashion, leading Baylor with 103 tackles along with 12.5 tackles for loss en route to first-team all-conference honors. An invaluable cog in Baylor's defense, Bernard stood out as one of the team's key leaders on and off the field across multiple coaching staffs. – Sam Khan Jr.

13 Brandon Smith
Penn State (6-3, 240)

Once a five-star prospect and the Gatorade Player of the Year in Virginia, Smith was a two-year starter at two different linebacker spots. Working at the Sam linebacker spot as a sophomore and at Will as a junior, Smith had flashes where his broad shoulders, explosiveness and freakish athleticism made him look like the next big thing on Penn State's defense. At other times, his tackling was questioned. Smith had four tackles for loss and no sacks or interceptions as a junior. He recorded 81 of his 132 career tackles in his third year and deflected five passes with one forced fumble. – Audrey Snyder

14   Darrian Beavers
Cincinnati (6-4, 252)

Beavers will tick a lot of boxes throughout the draft process. Beavers has NFL size and enough speed and athleticism to play sideline to sideline. He's a cerebral player as well, working at his pre-snap recognition as a fifth-year senior and flashing the instincts to make key plays around the ball in big moments. Returning for his bonus year of eligibility in 2021 proved wise, as he racked up 102 tackles (11.5 for loss), one interception, two forced fumbles and two recoveries for Cincinnati on his way to becoming a Dick Butkus Award finalist and earning first-team all-conference recognition. – Justin Williams

15   Mike Rose
Iowa State (6-4, 250)

The Cyclones' starting inside linebacker from his inaugural training camp in 2018, Rose opened 49 games at Iowa State and was the imposing and unquestioned leader for the Big 12's signature defense the last four seasons. Rose was named the Big 12 Defensive Player of the Year in 2020 and twice became a first-team All-Big 12 selection. In 2020, he earned first- or second-team All-American honors from four different outlets. Rose finished with 321 tackles, including 41 for loss, and six interceptions and missed only two games. – Scott Dochterman

Cornerbacks

1 Derek Stingley Jr.
LSU (6-1, 195)

Stingley will be remembered both as one of the best cornerbacks in LSU history and a strange what-if. He was an All-American as a true freshman during the 2019 championship run, and NFL teams told LSU he'd be the first corner taken if he could go pro at 18. But injuries plagued his next two seasons, only appearing in 10 games the rest of his college career and looking limited when he did. Still, Stingley is an uber-athletic corner built in a lab who has elite intelligence, too.
– Brody Miller

2 Ahmad Gardner
Cincinnati (6-2, 190)

A true lockdown cornerback, Gardner completely eliminated his side of the field at Cincinnati, to the point that he started blitzing more and more because opposing quarterbacks weren't even looking in his direction (he had three sacks in 2021). A consensus All-American in 2021, Gardner allowed just 131 yards against him all season and never gave up a touchdown in more than 1,000 coverage snaps during his three years with the Bearcats. – Justin Williams

3 Trent McDuffie
Washington (5-11, 195)

It took McDuffie three games to earn a starting cornerback spot as a true freshman in 2019, and he only got better from there. Opposing quarterbacks completed only 16 of 36 passes against him for 111 yards in 2021, per Pro Football Focus, with just 25 yards after catch and no touchdowns. Obsessive about fundamentals and technique, McDuffie is also a film junkie with a high football IQ. He has the skills to become the first Huskies DB picked in the first round since Marcus Peters in 2015. – Christian Caple

4 Andrew Booth Jr.
Clemson (6-0, 193)

Booth's athleticism made him one of the most electric cornerbacks in Clemson history. His one-handed 2020 interception in the end zone against a 6-foot-7 Virginia wide receiver will forever be the highlight of his Clemson career. Former Tigers defensive coordinator Brent Venables once compared Booth to a praying mantis for his length, and said in the fall Booth had to be the best tackling cornerback in college football. Booth, also known for his speed and physicality, earned first-team All-ACC honors in 2021. He finished 2021 with 39 tackles (three for loss), five pass breakups and a team-high three interceptions. – Grace Raynor

5 Kaiir Elam
Florida (6-2, 200)

The former four-star recruit from North Palm Beach earned All-SEC first team honors in 2020, collecting 39 tackles, two interceptions and 11 pass breakups for an 8-4 Gators squad that lost to Alabama in the SEC championship game. Elam, who made 26 career starts in three years at Florida, didn't earn any postseason recognition after the Gators finished 6-7 last season. He graded out 163rd out of 197 Power 5 cornerbacks in coverage (58.1 grade) according to PFF, despite giving up only 19 catches for 191 yards and two touchdowns and being targeted 36 times. – **Manny Navarro**

6 Roger McCreary
Auburn (6-0, 187)

McCreary probably would have started sooner had he not been behind current Miami Dolphins Noah Igbinoghene and Javaris Davis his first two seasons. When he replaced Igbinoghene in 2020 as Auburn's boundary corner, McCreary proved himself quite capable against great competition. Before he became a starter, McCreary got reps against the likes of Justin Jefferson and Ja'Marr Chase. As a starter, he had to face DeVonta Smith, John Metchie, Elijah Moore and Treylon Burks. McCreary will enter the NFL tested by the kinds of players he'll face in the league. – **Andy Staples**

7 Kyler Gordon
Washington (6-0, 195)

It took Gordon until his fourth college season to lock down a full-time starting job, but the athleticism was always there — he had the top vertical leap on the team from the moment he set foot on campus, and his quick twitch always suggested pro potential. In 2021, he put it all together, intercepting two passes, breaking up seven and finishing with the highest defensive grade on the team, per PFF, while earning first-team All-Pac-12 honors. He's also a physical tackler with a nose for the ball. – **Christian Caple**

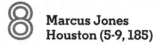

8 Marcus Jones
Houston (5-9, 185)

Jones did everything for the Cougars. The Paul Hornung Award winner was the nation's best returner (he recorded nine combined career kickoff and punt return touchdowns, including four in 2021), he shined at cornerback (his five interceptions were second-most in the FBS last season) and he even saw spot duty on offense, logging 10 catches for 109 yards and a score as a senior. Jones was an All-American at Troy before transferring to Houston and repeating those honors in each of his last two seasons. He was one of the most versatile and productive players in the country. – Sam Khan Jr.

9 Tariq Woolen
UTSA (6-3, 205)

A receiver early in his career, Woolen made the move to cornerback midway through his UTSA career. He played 11 games there (starting seven) as a junior and grew exponentially in his final season. In the nine games he was available in 2021, he broke up five passes, picked off a pass and compiled 25 tackles, including 2.5 for loss. He should test well upon arrival at the next level given his off-the-charts ability. – Sam Khan Jr.

10 Martin Emerson
Mississippi State (6-1, 202)

Emerson's first career start came against LSU in 2019. For a cornerback, facing a receiving corps led by Justin Jefferson and Ja'Marr Chase is the ultimate trial by fire. Emerson had to grow up quickly that season, but by 2020 he was one of the best cornerbacks in the SEC. Quarterbacks seemed to have an easier time throwing at Emerson in 2021. That might have something to do with QBs being less likely to throw at sophomore teammate Emmanuel Forbes, who likely will appear in this publication — with some very kind words from Dane Brugler attached — next season. – Andy Staples

11 Coby Bryant
Cincinnati (6-1, 191)

Despite the fact that he probably wasn't even the best cornerback on his own team (that would be Ahmad "Sauce" Gardner), Bryant still won the 2021 Jim Thorpe Award as the top defensive back in college football. He and Gardner combined to form the best cornerback duo in the country and led the Bearcats to the top pass efficiency defense rate in college football this past season. Bryant finished his five-year career at Cincinnati with nine interceptions, four forced fumbles and 35 pass breakups. – **Justin Williams**

12 Jalyn Armour-Davis
Alabama (6-1, 190)

After spending his first three years in Tuscaloosa redshirting and working on special teams, Armour-Davis got his chance to start at corner in 2021 and became a second team All-SEC defensive back on a team that went to the national title game. The large corner had three interceptions and several impressive tackles near the line of scrimmage, blowing up screens and run plays. – **Brody Miller**

13 Derion Kendrick
Georgia (6-0, 190)

Kendrick had a star-crossed three years at Clemson, where he began his career as a receiver (catching 15 passes for 210 yards on the national championship winner) then moved to cornerback and became an All-ACC selection. But he had discipline issues off the field, leading to his departure from the team after his junior year. Georgia took the chance on him, after waiting for a marijuana and traffic charge to be dismissed, and Kendrick was a model citizen and lockdown cornerback on the way to the national championship. – **Seth Emerson**

14 Cam Taylor-Britt
Nebraska (6-0, 205)

A standout from the start on a defense that improved incrementally in his four seasons, Taylor-Britt matched up physically against the best Big Ten receivers and showed a knack for timely playmaking. In Montgomery, Ala., he was a dynamic high school quarterback. A lack of defensive experience cost him major recruiting interest from SEC programs, though he turned down Auburn at the end for Nebraska and quickly validated the Huskers' faith. Taylor-Britt finished in Lincoln as the most complete player signed by Scott Frost in his first class of recruits. – **Mitch Sherman**

15 Mykael Wright
Oregon (5-11, 173)

Wright came in with big expectations as a top-50 recruit and played up to them in three seasons with the Ducks, earning Freshman All-America recognition in his debut season and first-team All-Pac-12 honors as a sophomore. Wright was a quality cover corner for the back-to-back conference champs and finished as their third-leading tackler in 2021. He also proved to be a dynamic player on special teams, delivering two kickoff return touchdowns as a true freshman. – **Max Olson**

Kyle Hamilton · S No. 1

Safeties

1 Kyle Hamilton
Notre Dame (6-3, 218)

Hamilton is a freak who made three interceptions in his first college practice and never let up, until a knee injury ended his Notre Dame career at midseason in 2021. He could have returned for the College Football Playoff but opted out of the lower-stakes Fiesta Bowl. He finished last season with seven passes defended (three INTs, four PBUs), which led Irish safeties despite playing just seven games. Hamilton could be a cheat code for an NFL defense considering the hashmarks are tighter in the pros than in college, which should let Hamilton be a single-high safety terror. – **Pete Sampson**

2 Daxton Hill
Michigan (6-0, 192)

Hill's career at Michigan had some ups and downs, but he persevered through scheme changes and a revolving door of position coaches to play productive football. A five-star recruit in the class of 2019, Hill is a versatile defensive back who can run like a corner and hit like a safety. The Wolverines used him extensively at nickel, a position that allowed him to showcase his versatility. He covers a lot of ground and made 69 tackles as a junior. – Austin Meek

3 Jalen Pitre
Baylor (5-11, 197)

After spending his early Baylor career at linebacker, Pitre blossomed in the "star" position (hybrid linebacker/safety) in two seasons under Dave Aranda. He became one of the most productive defenders in the country, a mainstay in opposing backfields and a factor in coverage. As a senior, Pitre led the Big 12 with 18.5 tackles for loss, fifth in forced fumbles (three) and seventh in pass breakups (seven). His speed and physicality made him an invaluable playmaker, earning him Big 12 Defensive Player of the Year in 2021. – Sam Khan Jr.

4 Lewis Cine
Georgia (6-1, 200)

The old adage that a safety leading the team in tackles is a bad thing didn't apply to Cine or Georgia this past season. The changing nature of the game was one reason, but Cine also made many of his 73 tackles on runs or short passes, a reflection of his nose for the ball. A highly ranked recruit out of Texas, Cine started two games as a freshman, then ascended to the strong safety role, which he locked down the past two seasons. – Seth Emerson

5 Jaquan Brisker
Penn State (6-1, 203)

A standout in the JUCO ranks at Scranton's Lackawanna College, Brisker's move across the state and into the Big Ten resulted in him becoming one of Penn State's most decorated safeties of all time. A team leader who toyed with leaving for the NFL Draft after the 2020 season, Brisker returned for the extra year and was voted a team captain, earned his degree and put together his best season. His 5.5 tackles for loss with two interceptions, five pass breakups and one fumble recovery made him an integral playmaker on a talented defense. – Audrey Snyder

6 Bryan Cook
Cincinnati (6-1, 204)

Cook was a bit of a late bloomer, starting his college career as an unheralded cornerback at Howard and then having to wait behind James Wiggins at Cincinnati. He only started one full season but quickly emerged as an instinctive, game-breaking talent in the secondary, with the ability to ball-hawk and cover tight ends and receivers but also come down in the box and stop the run. He had 96 tackles (five for loss), two interceptions and nine pass breakups as a first-team all-conference player in 2021. – Justin Williams

7 Kerby Joseph
Illinois (6-1, 200)

Joseph became just the fifth Illinois safety to earn first-team All-Big Ten honors in the last 50 seasons, and he was graded the nation's No. 1 defensive back in the regular season by PFF. He was the only player in the country to record at least five interceptions and recover at least three fumbles during the regular season. The Orlando, Fla., native finished the 2021 season with 57 tackles, one sack and two pass breakups. – Matt Fortuna

8 Nick Cross
Maryland (6-1, 215)

Cross had a big year in 2021, with career-highs in tackles (66) and interceptions (3) along with 3.5 tackles for loss, four pass breakups, three sacks and two forced fumbles. The safety is known for his agility and was one of the defensive leaders amid a bounce-back season in Mike Locksley's third season, a 7-6 campaign that ended with the Terps' first bowl win since 2010. Cross was a three-time all-Big Ten honorable selection. – **Nicole Auerbach**

9 Tycen Anderson
Toledo (6-2, 207)

Anderson played in 55 games over five seasons, working at both safety positions at the back of Toledo's defense. The Rockets finished last season first in the MAC in scoring defense, yards per play allowed and pass efficiency defense. Anderson missed last season's first three games with a knee injury – that included sitting out a closs loss at Notre Dame – but returned to help Toledo nearly win the MAC, with its three conference losses coming by a combined eight points. Anderson finished with 44 tackles, no interceptions and two PBUs. – **Pete Sampson**

10 Verone McKinley
Oregon (5-11, 196)

McKinley redshirted as a freshman and then put up three very productive seasons for the Ducks. He was a Freshman All-America in 2019 and led the team with four interceptions. He picked off one pass in the pandemic-shortened 2020 season and then led the nation in interceptions in 2021 with six. McKinley has a natural nose for the ball, and he's a willing hitter in run support. He also aspires to be the next Gus Johnson and always volunteered to be interviewed — even after Oregon's toughest losses. – **Andy Staples**

11 Alontae Taylor
Tennessee (6-0, 192)

The former high school quarterback and receiver flipped to corner in his freshman season and became a four-star starter for Tennessee and one of the team's most vocal leaders. He plays physical and still has plenty to learn about the position. He was productive despite his relative inexperience, turning one of his two picks in 2021 into a touchdown and breaking up six more passes, all career highs. He has good size, good speed and quickness that allows him to excel in man or zone coverage. – David Ubben

12 Leon O'Neal Jr.
Texas A&M (6-1, 203)

The spirited, charismatic safety improved every year on campus. He grew from a boom-or-bust player who made big plays mixed in with big mistakes as a youngster into a mature, disciplined safety who consistently did his job and emerged as a defensive leader as a senior. O'Neal was an effective, oft-used weapon on blitzes by defensive coordinator Mike Elko. His hard-hitting nature made him an asset against the run and in the open field. In coverage, he went from a liability as a sophomore and junior to an asset as a senior. – Sam Khan Jr.

13 Dane Belton
Iowa (6-1, 205)

Belton alternated between the Hawkeyes' cash position and strong safety when the defense flipped from 4-3 to 4-2-5, and he adjusted to play at an All-Big Ten level. At cash, Belton covered slot receivers and tight ends while handling run support near the line of scrimmage. At strong safety, Belton often played deep in half or quarters coverage. Belton, who started 26 games in three seasons, tied for the Big Ten high with five interceptions in 2021. He also broke up seven passes, recorded five tackles for loss and was credited for three quarterback hurries. – Scott Dochterman

14 Markquese Bell
Florida A&M (6-2, 200)

The FCS All-American hard-hitting safety from Bridgeton, N.J. is looking to become the first FAMU player drafted since Brandon Hepburn, a seventh-round pick of the Lions in 2013. He led the Rattlers with 95 tackles and five forced fumbles in 2021 and had one interception. In 2019, Bell registered 61 tackles, two forced fumbles and five interceptions in his first season in the MEAC. A 2017 Under-Armour All-American who signed with Maryland out of high school, Bell transferred to Coffeyville (Kan.) Community College. He played in eight games there, totaling 52 tackles with two interceptions in 2018. – Manny Navarro

15 Smoke Monday
Auburn (6-2, 204)

The former Under-Armour All-American from Atlanta started 25 games in his college career, earning All-SEC Second Team honors in 2020 and producing 171 tackles with five interceptions and five pass breakups over his career. He made his mark as a run stuffer and hitter but was often beaten in coverage on play-action plays. According to Pro Football Focus, Monday gave up 22 catches for 255 yards and for two touchdowns the 32 times he was targeted in pass coverage in 2021. – Many Navarro

Jake Camarda - P No. 2

Specialists

1 Matt Araiza
Punter, San Diego State (6-2, 200)

Araiza earned the nickname "Punt God" this past season and declared early for the NFL Draft, which says a lot for a punter. Araiza averaged 51.19 yards per punt, which is an NCAA record, and became a major weapon for an SDSU team that was defined by its defense and special teams. Araiza consistently gave the Aztecs an edge in the field position battle and closed one of the best punting seasons in NCAA history by earning MVP in the Aztecs' win over UTSA in the Frisco Bowl. Araiza also handled kicking duties for SDSU, which only added to his case as one of the most valuable players in the country. – Antonio Morales

2 Jake Camarda
Punter, Georgia (6-1, 191)

Camarda came to Georgia as the heir apparent to Rodrigo Blankenship at placekicker but ended up being the punter for four years, and a very good one. Other than the occasional shank early in his career, Camarda's leg was often a difference-maker, and his punts in the first half of this year's national championship bought time for the Georgia offense to get things together. Camarda thought about turning pro after the 2020 season, but it was a good thing for both him and the team he did not. – Seth Emerson

3 Cade York
Kicker, LSU (6-1, 200)

York may go down as the best kicker in LSU history, the one who became a steady rock during LSU's 2019 title run while leading the SEC in points before leading the SEC with 18 field goals in 2020. One of those 18 was the famous record-breaking 57-yard field goal through a dense fog to shock Florida in The Swamp. York made his third consecutive All-SEC team in 2021 while going an absurd 5 of 7 from 50-plus yards. He's the rare kicker to go pro after his junior year, because he had little left to prove. – Brody Miller

4 Cameron Dicker
Kicker, Texas (6-0, 219)

"Dicker the Kicker" proved a special teams force from the moment he stepped onto the Forty Acres. He notched a game-winning field goal against rival Oklahoma as a true freshman, showing his poise under pressure. He remained consistent throughout his career, connecting on 76 percent of his field goal attempts. He handled kickoff duties for most of his Texas tenure. As a senior he added punting to his repertoire, earning first-team All-Big 12 honors at that position while also connecting on 13 of 15 field goals in 2021. Whatever the Longhorns asked of Dicker, he did well. – Sam Khan Jr.

5 Jordan Stout
Punter, Penn State (6-3, 205)

Once a walk on at Virginia Tech, Stout entered the transfer portal in 2019 and sought a scholarship elsewhere. Penn State quickly scooped up the combo specialist who would become a Ray Guy Award finalist as a senior. Stout's big leg allowed him to handle all punts, field goals, kickoffs and extra points his senior season. He was a touchback machine with 59 of his kicks resulting in touchbacks. Stout punted just two seasons at Penn State but excelled as a senior, averaging 46 yards per punt with 25 of his 65 punts traveling 50 yards or more. – Audrey Snyder

6 Gabe Brkic
Kicker, Oklahoma (6-3, 200)

A 2021 Lou Groza Award finalist, Brkic is one of the most decorated, prolific and accurate placekickers in Oklahoma football history. He made 82.6 percent of his career field goal attempts, which ranks second in school history. In 2019, he was 17 for 17, marking the only perfect field-goal season in OU history that included 10 or more attempts. Brkic made nine field goals from 50 yards or more. He didn't miss any of his 160 extra-point attempts until his final game as a Sooner — Oklahoma's 47-32 Alamo Bowl win against Oregon. – Jason Kersey

7 Cal Adomitis
Long snapper, Pitt (6-1, 234)

The 2021 winner of the Patrick Mannelly Award, given to the top long snapper in the FBS, and an AFCA first-team All-America honoree, Adomitis snapped in 64 consecutive games during his collegiate career. Handling both long and short snapping duties, the Pitt captain bypassed an invite to the Senior Bowl after the 2020 season and returned to Pitt, where he became the school's most accomplished long snapper and ended his collegiate career by handling snapping duties for five consecutive seasons. – Audrey Snyder

Player
Profiles

Ikem Ekwonu
Sauce Gardner
Malik Willis
Kenny Pickett
Drake London

No. 1 pick candidate Ikem Ekwonu's quiet rise as 'the most feared offensive lineman in the ACC'

By Bruce Feldman

There was no NC State offensive lineman to be found on the 2020 All-ACC first team. Not on the second team, either. But last spring Ikem Ekwonu had his name on the lips of rival coaches around the league who consistently found themselves sidetracked during discussions of 2021 NFL Draft prospects by their praise of a 6-foot-4, 325-pound Wolfpack sophomore who wouldn't be eligible for another year.

"That guy reminded me of (former Louisville/New York Jets first-round offensive tackle) Mekhi Becton," said one ACC defensive coach of Ekwonu. "He's not as big, but he was steam-rolling people. He's probably nastier than Becton."

"To me, he's the most feared offensive lineman in the ACC," said an offensive line coach in the conference. "He's similar to Becton but more of an interior guy. He's got so much short-area power and explosiveness. He's violent. You'd go watch him on film: 'Oh, wow, he's destroying people.' He's got something in him that is not coached. There is some natural aggression and ferocity with the way he finishes and strikes. That is a gift."

And don't get Ekwonu's coach at NC State, Dave Doeren, started about his top lineman only making the All-ACC third team.

"His motor is really rare," Doeren said last offseason. "He is a very, very aggressive player. He is good, man. I mean, he is really good. I was shocked that he wasn't all-conference last year. I watched a lot of film, and there's nobody on offense that we have played that is as violent as he is as a blocker.

"How was he not first-team all-league? I have no idea. I thought we didn't play anybody like him?"

Vindication arrived in 2021, when Ekwonu shined for a Wolfpack team that finished 9-3, comfortably landing first-team All-ACC honors with the highest vote total of any offensive lineman in the conference. Now he's in the discussion to be the No. 1 pick in the 2022 draft, backing up the high praise that has marked his quiet rise.

Ekwonu finished his freshman season in 2019 as the Wolfpack's starting left tackle but began the 2020 season at left guard before he was moved back to left tackle for their game against Duke — the coaching staff was worried about the Blue Devils' standout defensive end Victor Dimukeje. Ekwonu graded out at 90 percent for the game, won co-ACC Offensive Lineman of the Week honors and never looked back.

"We wanted our matchup on their matchup and he dominated that kid," Doeren said, "and he ended up staying at tackle for the rest of the season."

Coaches say Ekwonu displays rare explosiveness and athleticism. NC State strength coach Dantonio Burnette says Ekwonu hit 18 MPH on the GPS last spring at practice, an impressive number for someone his size. He also says Ekwonu will run as fast as former Wolfpack first-round offensive lineman Garrett Bradbury, who clocked a 4.92 40 at the NFL Combine.

At NC State, Doeren makes a big deal about the number of "pancake" blocks his linemen make. At Sunday team meetings, Doeren will award a bottle of syrup for the team leader as he shows the team clips. Ekwonu led the team with 50 pancake blocks and with 22 knockdowns in 2020.

"You could probably stock a grocery store with all of the syrup that we've given out to him," said Doeren.

Ekwonu feels like he was short-changed, actually, on his pancakes, and thinks he actually had 60 that season. His favorite blocks of the campaign: The first, one against Miami on the Pack's opening drive, where he trucked Canes safety Bubba Bolden to clear the path for a touchdown at the end of a trick play.

"It really started the game on the note I wanted to start the game on," Ekwonu said. His other favorite: A pancake block on a wide zone on a fourth-and-1 late in the game.

"It kind of sealed the game," said Ekwonu.

Seeing Ekwonu emerge as a dominant force has been eye-opening for some rival coaches. They knew the name Ekwonu, but that had more to do with his fraternal twin brother, Osita, a speedy linebacker rated as a four-star recruit who plays for Notre Dame. Ickey was a three-star prospect.

"We didn't offer him, and we certainly regret it," said one ACC head coach. "He was just really raw. But you watch him now, and he's so athletic and tough. He plays with an edge and has really good feet. Credit to NC State. They were probably the only ones (in the ACC) that really wanted him. Everybody wanted his brother."

The Ekwonu brothers transferred to Charlotte's Providence Day from Weddington High (Matthews, N.C.) when they were freshmen. Their athleticism and drive comes from their parents. The twins' dad, Tagbo ("T.J."), is a doctor who stands 6-foot-6 and came to the United States from Nigeria, where he played college basketball. Their mom, Amaka, was a high school track star.

Amaka Ekwonu could see the difference in her twins' personalities from the time they were babies. Ikem, at birth, was stretching his neck, like he always wanted to see what was going on, she said. In elementary school, he won an award for joy.

"He is always happy," she said. "He just lightens the mood everywhere he goes. He is such a joker and has this happy spirit. Osi is a lot more reserved, a lot more like my husband. Ickey is a clown. To play with that aggression, it seems out of character for him. What I do know for sure, is that it has to be from God."

In that regard, he is aptly named for someone who plays and approaches everything the way he does. Ikem (pronounced ee-kem) means "my effort will not be in vain." The Ekwonus chose that name from the book "Things Fall Apart" by Nigerian author Chinua Achebe. Ikemefuna, Ekwonu's given first name, is one of the heroes of the story. The meaning of Osita's name loosely translates to "your day is coming," according to T.J. Ekwonu. Osi is a reserve defensive end at Notre Dame.

But in high school, it was Ickey — who got that nickname because his Pop Warner coach thought he resembled former Cincinnati Bengals running back Ickey Woods — hoping for a breakout.

"Ickey probably weighed 220 pounds. He moved pretty well but was just a little awkward, kinda goofy," said Otis Moore, who coached him on the defensive line and became a mentor. "He had a really good sense of humor and liked to clown around."

Osi Ekwonu started for four years at Providence Day. Ekwonu played mostly on junior varsity until his junior year. He knew big FBS programs were very interested in his brother.

"It was challenging, but something at my school, our coach, Coach (Adam) Hastings always taught us, was to have a chip on your shoulder, just play with a chip," Ekwonu said.

Ekwonu, who always seems to have a big smile away from the field (and even sometimes while he's playing in games), never really talked about any frustration he had from the recruiting process, but Moore knew it was there. Every morning Ekwonu would come into the football office to hang out.

"He never actually told me he was discouraged," Moore said. "He wasn't that type of kid, but I knew what was in him and that something was bothering him. You could see in his face that he was discouraged, wondering if he was ever gonna get any offers."

Moore's message was often the same: Be calm. Relax. Keep your head up. Your time will come.

"Use anything going on in your life and just play with it," said Ekwonu. "I definitely felt disrespected and I definitely use that as my motivator even to this day. I'm just trying to get my respect from people, leaving a mark on every team I play and everybody I face, so that people know my name."

Ickey first began to shine as a wrestler. The skills he honed on the mat — leverage, discipline, thriving in one-on-one situations — carried over to the football field as his body continued to develop. He emerged as a starter on both sides of the ball as a lineman on varsity in his junior year. His first offer came from Charlotte that season and later Appalachian State and some FCS programs.

"In that same time, my brother picked up Alabama, Notre Dame and Louisville — he got, like, seven offers in one day," said Ekwonu. "I was always happy for him, but I used it as motivation, like, alright, I need to make a name for myself too."

He also heard more from a handful of other Power 5 programs who began to show some interest. T.J. Ekwonu, the twins' father, said Ickey saw through some of those recruiters' intentions.

"He definitely had some coaches pretend to want him for his brother," T.J. Ekwonu said. "Ikem is very smart. He could see that and shake it off: 'I'm gonna work hard on my craft and show that you guys missed out on me.'"

Ekwonu continued to blossom on the field and in wrestling, where he won a state championship. His high school coaches marveled at the kid's physicality as a two-way lineman. They weren't sure what college coaches would see him better suited for but were convinced he was a special talent. They sent out all sorts of videos to college coaches showcasing Ekwonu's athleticism and his tenacity.

"We thought, hey, you may not know if he's an offensive lineman or a defensive lineman, but I want you to see just how nasty he plays, so here's (some) video of him, driving people 20-30 yards down the field," said Hastings, Ekwonu's head coach at Providence Day. "Trying to get that aspect of him to the colleges was really imperative."

Hastings and Moore's shrewdest recruiting move, though, was sending some cell phone video they scrambled to get from Ekwonu's impromptu performance as the anchor man in a relay race on the track to every college program and recruiting service they could think of. His football coaches had challenged him that another football player was faster than him, and Ickey kept telling them he was gonna show him.

"I knew he was fast, but I didn't know he was that fast 'til he got on that track," said Moore. "It was a shocker."

The other crazy thing about Ekwonu stepping in to run that relay race? He didn't even have running shoes. He borrowed someone's red high-tops.

"As he starts running, I said, 'Go get your phone out.' We need to film this, because he was about to track someone down from about 50 meters away," said Hastings. "The other guys were so far ahead of him and he just turned it on. It was like the Olympics when you see guys track people down, except he was 285 (pounds). It was one of those things when you see it happening, you're like, 'Oh, this is special. We've just captured in an eight-second video what we know is special about this kid.'"

Ask Dwayne Ledford, the O-line coach at NC State who signed Ekwonu, about when he knew he had something special in the three-star recruit, and that relay race is the first thing that comes up.

"I was like, 'Man, look at that! Watch him open up and run,'" Ledford said. "I was like, this kid can fly."

Ledford, who never got to coach Ekwonu because he left NC State to become the offensive coordinator at Louisville for two seasons before going to the NFL, already was sold on him.

"He had great length and is a very smart kid who is a great student from an outstanding family. His film was really good. You could see how flexible he was and that he could bend really well. Plus, he wrestled and was very good at it — and he liked it. But then he runs the anchor in a relay? I was like, What else could this kid do? I just thought the world of him from an athletic standpoint."

For Doeren, it was a different "wow" moment. The lineman had already committed to NC State, having done so the summer before his senior year. Doeren went to one of his high school games and was impressed that Ekwonu not only never came off the field but played hard every single snap.

"He was so violent," said Doeren. "There was a play where they threw an interception, and he ran the guy down. He just exploded on the guy. It was as hard a hit as I've seen in person. I was like, this guy's unreal. I came back and told our staff, 'This guy will start as a freshman as an O-lineman.'"

Ekwonu made his head coach look very prescient when the lineman earned freshman All-American honors in 2019 and became NC State's first true freshman to start at offensive tackle in nine years.

Doeren describes Ekwonu as a "thermostat" guy: "He definitely changes the temperature of the room. He's very upbeat. He brings a lot of energy to the group. He brings it to practice, brings it to everything that we do; not just with his style of play, but with his demeanor and attitude and the way he spreads it around to the guys around him."

Ekwonu isn't the first football standout whose affable, pleasant personality belies the nastiness of which he plays with on the field.

"I just love playing football, if I'm being real," he said. "So, I just give it 110 percent and I think it shows on the field: attack everything 'till the whistle blows. I've been playing with that mindset since Pop Warner. That's just always been my personality. Give everything 110 percent."

Ikem's own story is quite a tale for recruiters and NFL scouts. And yes, it's also one that seems to be giving a lot of rival coaches nightmares.

Cincinnati cornerback Sauce Gardner just might be the most bored player in college football

by Justin Williams

Asked last fall which team had tested him the most in the 2021 season, Sauce Gardner paused to think.

"Uh, probably Navy?" said Cincinnati's All-American, lockdown cornerback. "That's facts, yeah."

It's hilarious and telling that the pass-averse, triple-option Midshipmen — who fell behind against the Bearcats in the second half and had to sling it far more than usual in their Oct. 23 matchup — first came to mind for Gardner this season. The junior defensive back said there was another game when the opposing head coach came up to him afterward.

"He told me, 'Our job is just to stay away from you,'" Gardner said. "It made me realize that's probably how other schools are thinking."

The advanced metrics back up that thinking. According to Pro Football Focus, Gardner was one of 32 FBS cornerbacks who have been on the field for at least 450 coverage snaps this season (Gardner logged 480). None were targeted as the primary defender fewer times than Gardner, who saw only 40 targets in 14 games.

Those same metrics also provide an explanation: On those 40 targets, Gardner allowed only 20 receptions for 131 yards and zero touchdowns. In fact, in more than 1,000 career coverage snaps during his three seasons at Cincinnati, Gardner did not give up a single touchdown pass. His defensive pass efficiency allowed as the primary defender in 2021 (62.5) led FBS cornerbacks and his 6.6 yards per reception allowed ranked third. Even when opposing teams did try to throw against him — and they very rarely did — Gardner didn't cede much ground.

"I just take every play one at a time," said Gardner, who finished the season with 40 tackles and three interceptions. "Whenever I get bored and zone out, that's when the ball will get thrown at me. So I have to stay focused every play."

(For what it's worth, PFF disagrees with Gardner's assessment of Navy and lists East Carolina as targeting him the most this season. PFF charted seven targets by the Pirates, with Gardner allowing three receptions for 15 yards.)

The Detroit native had plenty of hype entering this season, but he didn't fully realize just how little action he was likely to see until the Notre Dame game on Oct. 2, with Fighting Irish defensive coordinator Marcus Freeman and cornerbacks coach Mike Mickens on the opposite sideline. The former Bearcats assistants recruited and coached Gardner at Cincinnati. There are few, if any, coaches out there who understand his capabilities better than those two, so if there were any weaknesses to exploit in Gardner's game, they would know.

"I had Notre Dame in my mind because they like their guys, and they're really not going to change nothing because of me," Gardner said.

Instead, Notre Dame threw at him only three times, according to PFF. Gardner allowed two receptions for 9 yards and had an interception.

To his credit, Gardner insists that he is not bored and not discouraged by how little he's tested. He understands that the lack of targets is a sign of respect and representative of everything he has worked toward since he arrived in Clifton as a lanky, underrated three-star recruit in the 2019 class. He also knows that NFL scouts and talent evaluators will recognize the same thing, regardless of the raw stats.

"It's not really frustrating because I know those clips where teams are not really going toward me or looking toward me, those clips are still going to be evaluated. So I have to treat every rep the same," Gardner said. "That's what I focus on and lock in on: not getting complacent. Scouts know what it is. There's a reason teams are not really trying to target me."

That message has been reiterated by the Cincinnati coaching staff, including head coach Luke Fickell, who said he talked to Gardner before the season about Shawn Springs, a former teammate of Fickell's at Ohio State. The veteran Pro Bowl and All-Pro NFL cornerback didn't have a single interception during his final season with the Buckeyes in 1996, but Springs still won Big Ten Defensive Player of the Year and was a consensus All-American.

"Because people recognized what he did. As good as he was, teams didn't challenge him a ton," Fickell said. "At that position, in particular, that's why it's really difficult, maturity-wise. It takes a unique individual."

Gardner also had the benefit of getting consistent work during the week in practice, where he regularly matches up against fellow NFL talent in wide receiver Alec Pierce and quarterback Desmond Ridder. Gardner might strike fear into opposing QBs, but on the practice field, Ridder doesn't shy away from him.

"When we're going to work, I go at him. When it's him and (Pierce) in the red zone, I'm going at Sauce. It doesn't just make the receiver and Sauce better, but it makes me better as well," Ridder said. "To everyone else, he's a big-time guy and all this and all that, but I do my best to keep him humble and keep him where he's at."

That midweek culture helped cultivate arguably the best cornerback in college football. Gardner's workout and practice habits initially caught the eye of Cincinnati coaches on the recruiting trail, and his work ethic hasn't changed in three years with the Bearcats. It's how he developed from a gossamer-thin, 6-foot-3, 160-pound prospect into a 200-pound first-round talent, and he continues to get better. Last offseason, cornerbacks coach Perry Eliano challenged Gardner to improve his tackling, particularly against the run. Gardner responded with a 77.8 PFF grade against the run, fifth highest among cornerbacks in the AAC. He registered the first of his three sacks last season against Tulsa, aided by the fact that the quarterback barely glanced in his direction.

His most notable tackle of the season actually came on a 51-yard gain for UCF, when Gardner chased down speedy receiver Ryan O'Keefe on an end-around to save a touchdown, flashing impressive speed and acceleration, as well as admirable effort.

"The guy who had the ball runs like a 10.4 in the 100 meters. He probably would have scored. But I felt like I was going to catch him," Gardner said. "I definitely didn't want to watch him, just spectate. I knew I got faster, but I had to test it."

With a name like "Sauce" and skills like that, Gardner has become a household name in college football. Yet for a player with a bright, lucrative future at the next level, at a position known for having outsized personalities, and one who regularly wears a diamond-crusted necklace sporting his famous nickname, he's surprisingly humble and reserved. It takes some provocation to draw out that earned confidence, like when Fickell wryly suggested that Gardner's fellow cornerback and close friend Coby Bryant is the better blitzer of the two, to which Gardner responded, "Eh, I like me, you know what I'm saying?"

Or when it was suggested to Garder that even the best cornerbacks are bound to give up a big play at some point.

"I'm a go-getter. Some cornerbacks have the mindset that receivers will make plays sometimes, and that's the life of being a corner. But me, I don't want the receiver to make no plays," he said. "I want to be on them every single play. I feel like that's where I separate myself from a lot of guys."

Gardner certainly has distinguished himself, a reality that should become even more evident this spring. But Cincinnati's shutdown cornerback never allowed himself to be distracted by all of that, rather focusing on his every-play mentality. He knows that even if quarterbacks aren't looking his way, someone is always watching.

"I don't think about the cause and effect of it. I just stay locked in," he said. "That's all that matters. I'm going to be prepared for whatever."

How Malik Willis of Liberty became one of the hottest QB prospects for the NFL Draft

by Jeff Howe

Tucked in an old Virginian town between the foothills of the Blue Ridge Mountains and the banks of the James River, on a campus light on football tradition, the NFL Draft's most electric quarterback prospect is redirecting the spotlight.

Malik Willis has become a superstar at Liberty University and a must-see showcase on the scouting circuit. He's got a chance to run the fastest 40 time at the combine for a quarterback in years, and he'll have one of the strongest arms in the NFL from the moment he's drafted.

Yet Willis was hardly recruited in high school. He barely played at Auburn for two years before transferring, and no one from the Power 5 conferences showed any interest before he chose Liberty.

His rise has been as unpredictable as it is spectacular.

Willis helped head coach Hugh Freeze turn Liberty into an overnight sensation. Now he has a chance to be the first quarterback selected in the 2022 draft.

"I was just doing what I thought I could do," Willis told The Athletic during a wide-ranging conversation from Liberty's football facility. "I just went out there and played and had fun. I feel like that's what I've got to continue to do. I can't focus on what people think."

'I needed to take it more seriously'

Willis' patience was tested as a high school recruit in Atlanta.

He was stuck behind upperclassmen until midway through his junior season at Westlake High, a famed football powerhouse and Cam Newton's alma mater. After Westlake dropped to 3-2 in 2015, the coaches finally rolled with Willis, who ripped off seven consecutive wins.

Heads began to turn, ever so slightly.

That spring, Willis committed to Virginia Tech as an athlete – he'd either play quarterback, receiver or cornerback. Jackson State was the only other program with an offer.

"I wasn't highly recruited, but it's all good," Willis said. "I used to get mad. I used to be like, 'I'm making all these plays. Where are my (recruiting) stars?' Everything happens for a reason."

He transferred across the county to Roswell High, which vowed to prominently feature him in the offense to magnify his recruitment. It worked, as Willis passed for 2,562 yards, rushed for 1,033 yards and accounted for 37 touchdowns for a team that lost in overtime of the state championship due to a missed field goal.

"Sick to this day," Willis interjected.

After that, Auburn went all-in on Willis as a quarterback, so he flipped his commitment to the Tigers. He'd have a chance to play at the program where Newton won the Heisman Trophy and a national championship.

Willis' time had come.

Until it didn't.

He was relegated to mop-up duty for two seasons and was only allowed to run a bare-bones version of the playbook. In that time, Willis was 11 of 14 for 69 yards and a touchdown, and he ran 28 times for 309 yards and two scores.

Nevertheless, Willis has since become accountable for his lack of playing time. He understands it was on him alone.

"I focused so much on my development physically that I just leaned on all my talents too much," Willis said. "I wasn't working as hard as I could outside of football. I wasn't caring about school because I was just trying to go to the league. I wasn't caring about watching extra film. Whatever I do, they're going to have to stop me regardless. But that's not how you play the position. That's not a true leader and a true quarterback. I just had to figure out that stuff for myself. People are going to say what they want. I needed to put in more effort. I needed to take it more seriously."

Reality didn't hit until Auburn's 2019 spring game, when Willis was 9 of 10 for 85 yards and a touchdown against the starting defense.

First, a coach told him it was a nearly perfect performance. Next, Willis was informed the starting competition that fall would come between freshman Bo Nix and redshirt freshman Joey Gatewood.

Willis was going to be a third-stringer as a junior.

"I was like, 'You just said I had a perfect game. You feel me? What just happened?'" Willis said. "But I wasn't doing the little things properly. It's more than what you do on the field. How are (my teammates) going to be behind somebody who is not going to be in there watching the film and holding other people accountable more than themselves? I'm just like, show up and do your job. That's what I was thinking. I was more of a 'me' person. I just needed to grow into a 'we' person."

That was essentially the moment Willis realized a quarterback's responsibilities extend far beyond the field. To get his journey back on track, he'd have to transfer.

'That might be the dude right there'

Liberty, tucked halfway between Washington D.C. and Charlotte, N.C., became a full-time FBS member in 2019 and had been investing major resources into the program. At that point, Liberty had one FCS playoff appearance and seven NFL Draft picks (with a single first-rounder) since its inception in 1973.

Liberty was also in the process of a $25 million renovation to its facility when it hired head coach Hugh Freeze in December 2018. Freeze had a long history of running a successful offensive system at his prior stops, but he had been out of college coaching for nearly two years since resigning from Ole Miss due to NCAA and internal investigations into impermissible benefits and personal misconduct.

With Willis in the transfer portal, Freeze called his close friend, Auburn coach Gus Malzahn, to learn why he hadn't yet reached his potential. Malzahn raved about the quarterback – his humble personality, his energy, his beaming smile – so Freeze and Liberty offensive coordinator Kent Austin evaluated as much tape as possible on Willis.

But it was a chore.

"I didn't have any film," Willis said. "I wasn't a highly recruited guy. People just thought I could run the ball, I guess. They didn't let me throw it much at Auburn. I don't know why. Anytime I got in, I got the same play. I got like three plays. It's all good, though. ... But I did used to want to throw it."

Freeze and Austin studied Willis' 14 passes and 28 runs in garbage time. They scoured the internet for workout videos. They pulled his high school footage.

They recognized the common denominator.

"You're either naturally talented or you're not," Austin beamed.

Willis was worth it, so they pressed to get him to Lynchburg. Liberty competed against Georgia State, Troy and Western Kentucky, but the Power 5 schools weren't interested in the quarterback who was loaded with athletic ability but lacking in evidence that it would come to fruition.

Willis, who wears No. 7 because that's how many days it took God to create the earth, checked his Bible verse of the day during the morning of his visit to campus. It included, in part, "Where the Spirit of the Lord is, there is liberty." Coincidentally, he later spotted that verse on the wall of Liberty's football facility and decided on his destination.

Freeze and Austin took Willis and his father to a restaurant in downtown Lynchburg that night, and they were stunned to see Willis brought a notebook. He jotted down everything Freeze said during dinner and the remainder of the visit and studied it upon his return home to Atlanta. Unbeknownst to Freeze, just by that visit, Willis had already mastered the first two days of offensive installation by the time he enrolled at Liberty.

"I was trying to get a head start," Willis shrugged.

Austin added, "That's when I knew this guy was going to pay the price to prepare."

Willis had to sit out in 2019 due to NCAA transfer rules, but he needed the break.

"I was just so immature," Willis said. "I just needed a smack upside the head to kick me into gear. I had a whole year here to redshirt. That was me maturing as a leader, me maturing as a quarterback, watching that film, dissecting and seeing what I need to do, understanding what defenses are trying to do to us, their responsibilities, and still homing in on my body and mind and trying to get right physically, mentally and spiritually.

"I had to overcome some of my deficiencies. I always relied on talent, so I was a bad practicer. I hated practice. Then when I got here, I was just trying to focus on trying to get better at practice every day. I just had to learn how to practice and what it's really for. I used to feel like games got you more experience. Everybody is always talking about experience. But at the end of the day, you have to hone those things, so when the bullets start flying, you rely on what you practice. I had to learn that. I was trying to do that. I love practice now."

Willis used the redshirt year to master Freeze's system and, more importantly, get his fundamentals in check. While Freeze and Austin evaluated Willis as a naturally accurate passer, they noticed his hips fell out of whack in certain situations, and that impacted his arm motion and release point, particularly on throws to the left side of the field. Plus, Willis had to improve his movement behind the line, as his explosive jump cuts tended to affect the integrity of the pocket, which could sabotage the whole play.

"He is unbelievably coachable. He'll try anything you ask him to," Austin said. "Malik is very self-aware. He doesn't mask stuff. He doesn't hide behind excuses. He is very honest about himself."

Through it all, Willis offered glimpses of the future. He was a terror as the scout-team quarterback, with the coaching staff telling him to take it easy on the starting defense.

"Every week," Willis laughed.

Willis danced through the defense with ease, creating highlight after highlight at practice. They couldn't get near him when he ran, and they couldn't believe the velocity of his passes.

"I would hear the defense come back to the locker room like, 'This boy is tough,'" Liberty wide receiver Kevin Shaa said. "We knew we had something cooking up over there.

"I didn't want to say anything too early, but that might be the dude right there."

Willis missed the games. He craved the competition. He so badly wanted to feel the stadium atmosphere.

But he got his fix from tearing up his own defense and his coaches' positive feedback. Willis felt like he was building toward 2020.

"That's the best thing ever," Willis said of lighting up the defense in practice. "Some days, coach was like, 'Can you stop? We need some confidence going into this game.' That was funny. It was fun going against them."

It was a necessary step in Willis' evolution – one that he called "the best-worst time of my life." He grew as a person and a quarterback, and by default, as a leader.

Willis shook out the bad habits from Auburn. As Liberty prepared for the 2020 QB competition, the sentiment from the coaching staff could best be summed up in three words.

"I can't wait," running backs coach Bruce Johnson recalled thinking.

'Did that really just happen?'

They were hopeful, even eager.

But Willis' coaches couldn't have truly been prepared for what was to come. After all, Willis still had to beat out Johnathan Bennett and Chris Ferguson for the starting job, and the fall-camp competition lasted for a couple weeks until Willis distinguished himself in the team scrimmage.

The athleticism was obvious. The passing was improving with his quick, compact and effortless throwing motion. Willis just needed to prove that he could be consistent in that area.

"Did I hope he could be (the starter)?" Freeze said. "Because of the way he could run around and do things, yes. But you still have to prove you can be an adequate passer to win college football games.

"I witnessed him do a few things (as a runner in the scrimmage) and said he's the guy. There's no doubt. We're going to have to make him a passer because he can do so many things with his legs. Once we made that decision, his confidence (improved) in throwing."

There was one more test. Just before the season opener, Willis' father texted him about an article that ranked the nation's 130 starting quarterbacks.

Willis was No. 123.

"Are you going to prove them wrong, or are you going to prove them right?" his father texted.

"I was like, all right, let's go," Willis smirked.

Willis' first start was a statement. He rushed for 168 yards – still a career high – and three touchdowns in a 30-24 victory against Western Kentucky.

Malik Willis was ready for launch.

"As the season went on, we're like, hold on, we might have a Heisman candidate right here," Shaa marveled. "To be honest, it caught me off guard. I knew he was good, but how he did last year just caught me by surprise."

Willis completed 64.2 percent of his passes for 2,250 yards, 20 touchdowns and six interceptions in 2020. He led all quarterbacks with 944 rushing yards and 14 touchdowns despite missing a game with a dislocated elbow in his left, non-throwing arm. (Willis would have played through it, but Freeze opted to rest him against FCS opponent North Alabama.)

And with six consecutive wins to open the season, Willis led Liberty to a national ranking for the first time in program history – in just its second full-time FBS season. They finished 10-1, including a 37-34 overtime victory against No. 9 Coastal Carolina in the Cure Bowl, where Willis was 19 of 29 for 210 yards and two interceptions with 137 rushing yards and four touchdowns.

"It was a surreal year, one of my favorites in coaching," Freeze said. "Malik is a huge part of it. You don't win those 10 games without him. He definitely put himself on the map."

Word spread through the coaches' offices last offseason. Their 6-foot-1, 225-pound quarterback was a likely first-round draft pick. In a wide-open 2022 quarterback class, Willis' physical tools stood alone.

Freeze and Austin conducted video calls with a host of NFL teams last year. This season, Freeze said every team's scouting department has been through campus at least twice.

Willis opened the season on a tear, completing 71 percent of his passes for 1,105 yards, 11 touchdowns and no interceptions plus 418 rushing yards and six scores. The final game of that stretch was against UAB, as Willis had 144 rushing yards and two touchdowns along with 287 passing yards and a score.

Then he hit an uncharacteristically poor stretch with three interceptions in back-to-back games, including a stunning loss to Louisiana-Monroe.

Willis, sitting at a round table with two chairs inside a private room at the football facility, detailed all six interceptions. He used the air as his whiteboard – the coverages, the routes, what he could or should have done better. The mistakes consumed him.

The sixth pick hurt the most, as it thwarted a potential game-winning drive in the final two minutes against ULM. He knew there were two other open targets, but he gasped as he just missed a bigger play by several inches.

"That sucked," Willis said. "That hurt. I missed him by about six inches, man. Just a little high. I could have thrown it to the tight end or running back, but I learned from that. Each one, I'm going to learn from. I'm never going to blame it on somebody else. I threw them. It's all good. I've just got to learn from it. It's over. It's in the past. It just so happened they got thrown in clusters. That sucks. Yeah, I've got to take care of the football. That's how you win and lose games, the turnovers."

Willis responded from the slump with a performance Oct. 23 at North Texas that his team will never forget. He was sacked midway through the second quarter, and his tackle landed on his foot. It felt numb, and they feared it was broken.

Complicating the matter – or to add to the legend of it all, however the Malik Willis Reed story is told – the X-ray machine at the stadium was broken, so Willis was taken to the hospital across campus for an evaluation. Some of his teammates watched him walk out of the stadium, so they feared a disaster for their leader and NFL Draft hopeful.

Doctors determined it was a sprain, so Willis hustled back to the stadium and ask Freeze to get back in the game. Liberty trailed 26-14 with 7:27 remaining in the third quarter.

"Once they said it wasn't broken, I was like, 'Let's go play,'" Willis said. "They wrapped it up, and I was all good. I would feel so bad if I was just worried about myself and decided not to finish the game. I would feel so terrible if we would have lost that game if I didn't go back in there, so I had to go back in the game and see what happens. My adrenaline started pumping. I didn't feel anything."

Willis was 12 of 18 for 217 yards and three touchdowns. Liberty prevailed, 35-26.

"It gave us a boost of confidence," Shaa said.

"Our main dude is coming in, so we've got to go 10 times harder because we see what he's doing."

Add it to the list of highlights. Everyone has their favorite. Austin once counted eight defenders who missed a tackle in the red zone and ribbed Willis for not finding a way to scoot past the other three. Shaa actually dropped his favorite pass because he was so shocked Willis found a way to rope it through three defenders.

The list goes on as long as the internet highlights will allow.

"He does some freakish things," Freeze said. "You just look, like did that really just happen?"

Austin added, "Malik has made three or four plays since I've been here that I've never seen anybody make. Nobody else in the country can make those plays."

'I've still got so much in front of me'

Quincy Avery, who runs QB Takeover in Atlanta, has trained some talented quarterbacks, including Deshaun Watson, Patrick Mahomes, Trey Lance and Justin Fields.

Last offseason, Avery conducted a workout at Georgia Tech's indoor facility and wanted to test Willis' huge arm in a different way. They marched out to the 50-yard line to see if Willis could rocket a ball straight up into the 65-foot roof.

"He goes to the middle of the field at the highest point, leans back, launches one and it slams into the top of the ceiling," Avery said. "It could have gone 10-15 yards farther."

Avery has tried the exercise with others and never seen anyone else come close.

"I worked with Mahomes (for one weekend) going into his last year in college," Avery said. "I can say this very confidently: Malik has the strongest arm of anybody I've ever seen."

As for the speed, Willis ran a 4.37-second 40-yard dash as a sophomore at Auburn.

Is he faster now?

"I think so," he grinned.

Michael Vick and Robert Griffin III, who each ran a 4.33, are the only quarterbacks who have run a sub-4.4 40-yard dash at the scouting combine since 2000. So Willis has a chance to make history if he decides to run.

He'll undoubtedly dazzle with his arm. His personality will win over coaches and executives. And his accountability – why Willis left Auburn for Liberty and took the unconventional route into first-round consideration – will absolutely win over skeptical evaluators.

"I'm not going to lie to you," Willis said. "I try to be honest with myself. If not, it's going to eat me up. I'll be like, 'Dang, they're going to believe that.' I don't like lying, for real. It just makes me feel bad. My conscience talks loud. I just try to tell the truth. It made me who I am."

With the potential to be the first quarterback off the board, Willis by default has a chance to be the No. 1 overall pick. He'll be competing with Matt Corral of Ole Miss, Cincinnati's Desmond Ridder, Pittsburgh's Kenny Pickett and North Carolina's Sam Howell, and it's too early to project how the next five months will unfold.

"I've still got so much in front of me," Willis said. "You just can't be stuck on what can happen or what might happen in the future, or what had happened in the past. You learn from the past and try to put it in the present. You can't do anything with the future. It's too far away. We've got to see what happens after the year. What you put on tape is the truth at the end of the day. If I don't have any tape, how can I say I'm going to do this or that? I don't really think about it. It's cool that we're talking all this stuff about it."

"All the conversation stuff, it is what it is. That's people talking."

And Willis is the one playing. So frequently, it's been at such a high level that the NFL can't help but gush over his talent.

They're flocking to gaze at the league's next big prospect at Liberty – an unconventional spot for a player who traversed an unconventional path.

The NFL has found Malik Willis. He showed them the way.

Pitt savior Kenny Pickett's big year: an ACC title, a Heisman Trophy campaign and a wave of NFL Draft buzz

by Matt Fortuna

The birth of "Kenny Heisman," ironically enough, traces all the way back to Max Browne. Four years ago, Browne was something of a Heisman-caliber savior at Pitt, a former No. 1 quarterback prospect who left Southern California for Western Pennsylvania in hopes of a fresh start. When he went down with a shoulder injury in the sixth game of the season, plenty of thoughts went through coach Pat Narduzzi's mind.

The first: "Holy cow. He's out."

The second: "I'll never forget: I put my hands on my knees, I'm looking at Max Browne and in my head, I'm saying: Kenny Pickett is going to have to play. Period. And that was the faith we had in him just from scout team, his composure, the way he runs around. I just knew right then if we were going to win some football games to finish up the season, we were going to need Kenny Pickett.

"So Kenny gets mad at me, like, 'Why didn't you just start me?' But I didn't want to throw him out into the fire right away."

The true freshman Pickett didn't end up starting until the 2017 season finale against undefeated, second-ranked Miami. On Black Friday in the Steel City, he orchestrated one of the season's biggest upsets, putting a nice bow on an otherwise erratic 5-7 season for the Panthers and charting the course for a promising future to come.

Pitt won the ACC Coastal Division the following season ... but finished with a 7-7 overall record. The Panthers went 14-10 across the following two years, with Pickett putting up big numbers but the program zig-zagging, winning games it had no business winning (such as ending UCF's 27-game regular-season winning streak in 2019) only to face-plant in games it had no business losing (such as falling to Boston College in the regular-season finale that same year — one day before BC fired its coach).

The 2021 season looked the same and different all at once, the big change being that Pickett found another level and became a Heisman Trophy finalist, finishing third in the voting behind Bryce Young and Aidan Hutchinson. Pitt lost to Western Michigan in September, then won its first ACC title and earned a Peach Bowl berth, finishing 11-3. Now Pickett is in contention to be the first quarterback off the board in April.

Pickett completed 72 percent of his passes for 4,319 yards with 42 touchdowns and just seven interceptions. His 15 touchdown passes between Sept. 18 and Oct. 2 broke Dan Marino's 1981 school record for most touchdown passes across a three-game stretch. Pitt scored at least 40 points in five consecutive games, a school record. The Panthers finished third in the nation in scoring at 41.4 ppg.

"He's one of the greatest to ever suit up at the University of Pittsburgh and in the game of football in general, so hearing your name next to his and passing some of the things he's done in the past here, it's incredible," Pickett said of Marino. "It's special, and it's something you see on the recruiting visits. You see that Dan Marino played here, you see all the records he has and all the great things he's done and that's just kind of the guy you're chasing, so it's definitely special."

That Pickett is in position to do this is a byproduct of both good and bad timing. He played in four games in 2017, but because the NCAA's redshirt rule at the time covered only the season's first four games — and not any four games, as it does now — the 2020 season was set to be his last in a college uniform.

That would have been all well and good, as Pickett had started 36 games, earned a Senior Bowl invite and received feedback telling him he'd be a fifth-round pick in the NFL Draft.

Then the NCAA gave everyone an eligibility mulligan due to the pandemic. Even then, though, no one inside the UPMC Sports Performance Complex was sure what Pickett would do. Now, with his eye-popping 2021, Pickett has put himself in the Day 1 conversation.

"Everybody likes to go to the amusement parks and take the fast pass," Narduzzi said. "That's not always the best pass. Sometimes the ride feels better when you stand in line for a while when you get there.

"The great thing about Kenny is he never looked backward."

Pickett reflects on the kid who took over the offense against the resurgent Hurricanes in 2017 and laughs, barely able to recognize some parts of his game while knowing that little has changed about his overconfident demeanor.

He is, after all, a 6-foot-3, 220-pound son of a former All-American linebacker from Division II Shippensburg.

"I just play with an edge," Pickett said. "I feel like there's only one way this game can be played. It's not for nice guys. It's a violent sport. It's played by alpha individuals. And I feel like as soon as I step between those lines that I'm the best player on the field. You just have to have that edge. It's the only way I know how to play, so I just find the way to grow the chip on my shoulder is playing with even more of an edge every time I step out there."

Pickett took advantage of deregulated name, image and likeness rules to feed his offensive line, as the group had a weekly Tuesday dinner at The Oaklander, a local hotel, thanks to Pickett's profile. When Pitt had its letdown against Western Michigan, Pickett was part of a players-only meeting that focused on making sure that that would never happen again, promising that this season would be different from Pitt's recent past. Then he went out and put together a college career finale that has NFL evaluators hoping he can become the face of a franchise.

"He's a calm, cool, collected guy, but you know what he's saying has presence behind it, has meaning behind it," tight end Lucas Krull said. "He knows what he's going to say and everyone's listening and everyone feels what he says.

"He's not really going to scream at anybody; everyone has that respect for him where he doesn't need to. But when he's talking, everyone's up in their chairs, eyes are locked on him, everyone's listening to what he's saying. He's really just talking from the heart."

How far has Drake London come? Just ask the former dominant USC wideouts tearing up the NFL

by Antonio Morales

If anyone knows what a Biletnikoff Award-caliber receiver looks like, it's Michael Pittman Jr.

In his final season at USC, Pittman caught 101 passes for 1,275 yards and 11 touchdowns, challenging Robert Woods, Marqise Lee and JuJu Smith-Schuster for the title of most productive receiver in recent Trojans history. That effort made Pittman a finalist for the award given to college football's most outstanding receiver in 2019, and he hasn't slowed down since, notching 88 catches for 1,082 yards during a breakout second year with the Indianapolis Colts.

As he watched Drake London star for his alma mater from afar, Pittman was reminded of himself — with one exception.

"Shoot, the season that he's having is just going to blow mine out of the water," Pittman said. "He's going crazy. ... I will be shocked if he doesn't win the Biletnikoff."

His front-row ticket to college football's award circuit was derailed by a fractured ankle suffered after his second touchdown catch of an Oct. 30 win over Arizona, but London's stellar junior season was a beacon of excellence amid a bizarre season at USC, which included the firing of coach Clay Helton after just two games. In just eight games, he caught 88 passes for 1,084 yards and five touchdowns, showcasing the skill set that has NFL teams drooling. He finished 15th in the FBS in receptions and 28th in yards even after his competitors had all of November to catch him, and he did it all while being the only consistent receiving threat on USC's offense and the chief focus of defensive gameplans.

"Now, you just throw him the damn ball and he's gonna get it," Pittman said. "I've been watching him play, if I was (USC quarterback Kedon Slovis) I'd be throwing him the ball every single play."

Over the past decade, it seemed like whenever a great receiver arrived at USC, there was an exceptional one already on campus to help him get acclimated. When Lee got to campus, Woods was coming off a breakout freshman year. They were both there when Nelson Agholor joined the program. Smith-Schuster's freshman year was Agholor's junior season. And Pittman's freshman year overlapped with Smith-Schuster's final season.

As a freshman in 2019, London joined a receiver group that already had Pittman, Amon-Ra St. Brown (a fourth-round pick and rookie standout for the Detroit Lions in 2021) and Tyler Vaughns, who sits third on USC's all-time receptions list with 222.

"Really, (he learned) how to work and how to go about his business and compete, be a dog," said Keary Colbert, London's receivers coach at USC. "He had some great examples as a young guy, and they all took him under their wing, and he was fortunate enough to have that. The cool thing is to see him do that with some of the younger guys in the room, and he's doing it in the same way the older guys did it for him. That's what this place has been about for a long time."

London said he has taken different aspects of each mentor's game and tried to incorporate them into his. He admired Pittman's ferociousness, physicality and demeanor. Both players are excellent at high-pointing the ball and winning contested-catch situations. London said St. Brown took the field every day with a "Mamba-like mentality," so London went 100 percent at practice to the point where has to be held out to avoid risking injury. And he liked the smoothness of Vaughns' routes, which is something he worked on in 2021.

"If I could mold that all into one," London said, "I think that's like the perfect receiver in my eyes."

London might not be a burner, but he's fast enough. He also has a perfect combination of body control, hand strength, toughness and natural instincts.

St. Brown remembers the work London has put in to get to this point. He recalls a text he sent to London after the 2019 season. London had caught 39 passes for 567 yards and five touchdowns as a freshman but was still splitting time between football and basketball. St. Brown invited him to come to a receiver workout with him.

"I remember he told me he doesn't have a receiver coach," St. Brown said. "He'd never had a receiver workout in his life. He's never really done any drills. That was really kind of eye-opening to me. ... He came out and you could tell he was kind of uncomfortable because he had never really done the footwork drills or all that. But he hasn't really been exposed to it and he's been going off straight ability this whole time."

And Pittman's first impression of London?

"Who is this tall freshman that can't decide whether he wants to play basketball or football?" Pittman said. "He was really talented, but he wasn't just fully committed to playing football yet. So he would have some setbacks."

The loss to Washington that season sticks out. The Trojans had to start backup quarterback Matt Fink with Slovis in concussion protocol. London was targeted a few times but finished without a catch. Fink threw behind him on one first-quarter pass and was picked off. Then late in the game, with USC facing an important fourth-and-goal, Fink threw to London in the end zone, but he was covered tightly and couldn't come down with the catch. The Trojans neared the red zone again a few minutes later, and Fink targeted London again but left too much air on the pass. Another interception.

"He was really frustrated," Pittman said. "I just walked over to him and told him that he just has to take accountability for it. I told him we have to make (the quarterback) right, and from that week he started going off."

London went catchless again in USC's next game that season, against Notre Dame. From that point on, over the next 21 games until his injury, he caught 157 passes for 2,091 yards and 15 touchdowns. That averages out to over seven catches for nearly 100 yards per game.

"Now, I don't want to take credit for him being a monster because Drake is a monster," Pittman said. "But it clicked for him and from then on out, he was just a different player."

Pittman spent the early part of his career with Sam Darnold and Smith-Schuster, taking some lessons from the last quarterback-receiver connection to power a USC Rose Bowl campaign.

"(I learned) from those guys that it doesn't just happen," Pittman said. "You have to go take it, you have to sacrifice and everything comes at a price."

London's sacrifice came late last year when he decided to focus solely on football after playing at least two sports for his entire childhood and his first year of college. Cindi London, Drake's mother, described basketball as her son's first love, so deciding to set it aside and focus strictly on football was an emotional decision, but a smart one. Football was clearly his future.

That decision has clearly paid off. London carried the Trojans' passing attack in 2021, with more receptions than USC's next leading receiver, Tahj Washington, despite playing only eight games. Opposing defenses knew London was the focal point of the Trojans' offense, and he still managed at least nine catches in seven of his eight games.

"His craftiness in his route running. His route precision," St. Brown said. "His ability to get in and out of breaks. His understanding of defenses, I can tell when he first got there he didn't really know coverages, which is normal. Some high schools don't really teach that stuff. He's starting to understand football more, you could tell the way he's playing. Just the position as a whole, he's honed in on his craft."

London arrived at USC in the summer of 2019 as a four-star prospect somewhat overlooked within a recruiting class that featured receivers Bru McCoy and Kyle Ford, both top-100 players in the recruiting cycle. But McCoy and Ford couldn't practice during training camp that year for health reasons, which left a lot of reps to London.

Back then, London only impressed in flashes, Colbert said. The coaching staff knew the more reps London got, the better he'd become.

"I just think as he continued to work and finally stepped away from basketball and committed 100 percent to football, you saw him continue to reach toward his ceiling," Colbert said. "And I still think he has some room up there."

If London maintains this current pace as he returns to 100 percent and arrives in the pros, he'll end up joining his fellow Trojans with more lofty accolades.

Bruce Feldman's NFL Draft Freaks List

The 2022 draft prospects with the freakiest abilities and skills

Taⅰiq Woolen = No. 2

In the past, athletic freaks like Myles Garrett, DK Metcalf and Saquon Barkley have lived up to — and in many cases exceeded — the hype. Others from more off-the-radar college football programs, like Lenoir-Rhyne defensive back Kyle Dugger, have also blown up with their testing performances during the pre-NFL Draft process. As we ramp up to the 2022 draft, it's time to focus on the biggest freaks in this prospect class.

170 | 2022 NFL Draft Preview

1 Aidan Hutchinson
Michigan, defensive end

He was a dominant player for the Big Ten champions and really set the tempo for the Wolverines' breakout season. Expect the 6-foot-6, 265-pound Hutchinson to keep wowing people in the draft process. He's got the tools to vertical jump in the high 30s, run the 40 around 4.6 and put up one of the fastest shuttle times of anyone at any size, having clocked a 4.07 last offseason.

2 Tariq Woolen
UTSA, cornerback

His freakish athleticism was a well-kept secret last summer. Not anymore. Woolen measured in at 6-foot-3 1/2, 205 pounds with 33 1/2-inch arms at the Senior Bowl. He also has consistently hit over 23 mph on the GPS. He told The Athletic this month that he's been training this spring to broad jump over 11 feet (he's gone 11-5 previously in testing at UTSA), go over 40 inches in the vertical and run the 40-yard dash in 4.3 seconds. Those are eye-popping numbers, but they are even more remarkable given his size.

3 Evan Neal
Alabama, offensive tackle

Neal has rare flexibility and athleticism given his enormous frame; he has played at 6-foot-7, 350-plus pounds. Former Alabama director of sports science Matt Rhea calls Neal "the most impressive lower body power athlete we have ever seen. His jumping power is in the top one percent we have ever measured." Neal routinely hits box jumps at 48 inches, benches almost 500 pounds and almost topped 19 mph last summer on the GPS despite weighing 350 pounds.

4. Kyle Hamilton
Notre Dame, safety

As impressive as his workout numbers are, his film is even more impressive. He has uncanny range and the ability to make big plays from the deep middle, as evidenced by the ground he covered in picking off a pass in the season opener against Florida State that still has scouts' jaws on the ground. The 6-foot-4, 220-pounder clocks 21 mph on the GPS, has vertical jumped almost 42 inches and has a 10-8 broad jump.

5. Kalon "Boogie" Barnes
Baylor, defensive back

Barnes, a converted wide receiver, has legitimate big-time track credentials; The 5-foot-11, 183-pounder once clocked a 10.04 in the 100 meters and was a two-time Texas state 100- and 200-meter champ. There are a handful of folks in the training world who suspected he had a shot at breaking the combine 40 record of 4.22 seconds.

6. Tanner Conner
Idaho State, wide receiver

The former standout hurdler on the Idaho State track team has terrific size (6-foot-3, 230 pounds) and wheels. He averaged almost 19 yards per catch the past two seasons. He vertical jumped 40 1/2 inches this offseason, broad-jumped 11 feet and has run in the 4.3s. There has been some skepticism about his route-running ability, but folks close to him expect him to win over doubters in change-of-direction drills. They also say his shuttle times will be just as strong as everything else he does, with a 4.2 shuttle and 6.8 L-drill very possible.

Bernhard Raimann = No. 7

7 Bernhard Raimann
Central Michigan, offensive tackle

He started playing for the Vienna Vikings in Austria as a 14-year-old before coming to Michigan as part of a high school exchange program. At Central Michigan, he began his career as a tight end and caught 20 passes before moving to the offensive line. Now at 6-foot-6, 304 pounds, Raimann has retained that pass-catching athleticism, having run a 1.56 10-yard split and also vertical jumping 33 inches and broad jumping 9-7 1/2. His shuttle at Central Michigan was 4.60. He also can put up a lot of reps on the bench, having maxed out at 450 pounds.

8 Travon Walker
Georgia, edge rusher

At 6-foot-5, 275 pounds, Walker is quite the specimen with great length (his arms are expected to measure around 35 inches). Some scouts think he could possibly run the 40 in the high 4.5s. On the field, he had six sacks and a team-high 36 quarterback hurries for the national champions.

9 Boye Mafe
Minnesota, edge rusher

He was just over 200 pounds when he arrived at Minnesota but measured in for the Senior Bowl at 6-foot-3 1/2, 255 pounds. He had a very good week in Mobile, Ala. He figures to do exceptionally well in the testing portion of the evaluation process. Mafe has vertical jumped 40 1/2 inches in training. In the past he's also broad jumped 10-6 and run the 40 in 4.57 seconds.

10 Leo Chenal
Wisconsin, linebacker

One of the big reasons behind the Badgers' stout defense was Chenal, the explosive linebacker who is expected to weigh in at 250-plus pounds. He has a chance to run a sub-4.6 40 to go with a 36-inch vertical, but it's his change of direction that may turn even more heads. He's expected to be around 7.00 in the L-drill and 4.10 in his 5-10-5 shuttle. Oh, and he also might get 40 reps of 225 pounds on the bench.

11 Ikem "Ickey" Ekwonu
NC State, offensive lineman

The most physically dominant lineman in this class, Ekwonu's film is one long masterpiece of offensive line brutality. He's also much more nimble than many have given him credit for. Expect him to weigh in at 315 pounds and still run the 40 in the 4.9s. He also benches 225 pounds in the 30-rep range.

12 Tyquan Thornton
Baylor, wide receiver

Boogie Barnes isn't the only Baylor player who has a decent shot of running the 40 in the 4.2s. The 6-foot-3, 185-pound Thornton, a 10.50 100-meter guy in high school, has been sub-4.3 in training.

13 Jason Poe
Mercer, offensive lineman

He was a Division II All-American at Lenoir-Rhyne before transferring to Mercer. The 6-foot-2, 300-pound Poe lacks ideal height but has ridiculous athleticism and is incredibly light on his feet. Poe is expected to run the 40 in the 4.8s. He has a vertical jump of 34 inches-plus. He's also benched almost 500 pounds and power cleaned almost 400. His broad jump will be in the 10-foot range and his shuttle in training has been 4.50.

14 Travis Jones
Connecticut, defensive tackle

The 6-foot-4 1/2, 326-pound powerhouse (7.5 TFLs, 4.5 sacks) has been the best thing UConn football has had going in a long time. He was once around 360 pounds but really worked on his body and got down to 13 percent body fat. He should get in the mid-30s on the bench and close to 30 inches on his vertical jump. Don't be shocked if he cracks 4.60 on his shuttle time. He did a 4.57 last offseason.

15 Daniel Faalele
Minnesota, offensive lineman

The biggest man in this draft — 6-foot-8, 387 pounds, 86-inch wingspan, 11-inch mitts — the huge Australian moves incredibly well for his size. He has vertical jumped 29 inches and broad jumped 8-7.

16 Kyler Gordon
Washington, cornerback

He's a solid 6-foot, 200 pounds with amazing body control and athleticism. A lot of that was honed with his background in dance, kung fu and ballet. Gordon's combination of burst and change of direction is reflected in a 42.5-inch vertical jump as well as a blazing 3.87 shuttle time while at Washington.

17 Trevor Penning
Northern Iowa, offensive tackle

The latest gem from the Missouri Valley Conference, Penning was a nasty force at the Senior Bowl, and he's much more than just a mauler. At 6-foot-6 1/2 with almost an 84-inch wingspan, he'll weigh around 325 pounds but may run the 40 in the 4.9s. He also has a good shot at running a sub-4.50 in the shuttle.

18 Jeffrey Gunter
Coastal Carolina, edge rusher

A former two-star recruit, Gunter was a disruptive force in the Sun Belt. He played in the mid-270s at 6-foot-4, but was down to 259 pounds for the Senior Bowl. His vertical jump stands out at 39 inches, as does a 4.37 shuttle he's timed. He's broad-jumped 10-2 while weighing in the 270s, so that should be impressive.

19 Derek Stingley Jr.
LSU, cornerback

He was sensational as a true freshman in the Tigers' 2019 national title season but was hobbled by an assortment of injuries the past two years. The old Tigers staff doesn't question his athleticism, but right now a lot of the expectations for his pre-draft workouts are tied to his amazing showing at Nike's 2018 Opening in Dallas. There, the five-star cornerback measured 6-foot-1 and 193 pounds, clocked a 4.30-second 40 time and had a 42-inch vertical to go with a 4.28 shuttle. It will be interesting to see what he does during the draft process.

Jeffrey Gunter = No. 18

20 Devonte Wyatt
Georgia, defensive lineman

One of the many Freaks on the Bulldogs' national title defense, the 6-foot-3, 305-pounder is expected to run in the 4.8s— he clocked a 4.87 last summer. The former high school shot-putter has vertical jumped 31 inches.

21 Tyler Linderbaum
Iowa, center

Whether it's a record-setting performance at the annual Solon Beef Days in Iowa, where he heaved a 60-pound hay bale 14 feet high, or pinning former Freaks king Tristan Wirfs on the mat, or dominating almost every opponent the Hawkeyes faced, the 6-foot-1, 290-pounder is an agile powerhouse. Expect him to shine in the draft process, just like he always does. At Iowa, we hear he'd run a 1.55 10-yard split and was timed at 4.22 in the shuttle, both numbers that would be good for a running back or defensive back.

22 Darrell Baker
Georgia Southern, cornerback

The 2016 Georgia high school long jump state champion has ideal size for corner at 6-foot 1/2, 198 pounds. He's put up some fantastic testing numbers at Georgia Southern, vertical jumping 43 inches and doing 10-11 in the broad jump. He's also run a 4.41 40.

23 Alec Pierce
Cincinnati, wide receiver

A 6-foot-3, 215-pounder who has a track and volleyball background, Pierce displays the toughness you'd expect from an athlete who also played linebacker at Cincinnati. Scouts love his ability to block. They'll also love his wheels. This is a player who is expected to run the 40 in the low 4.4s, jump over 40 inches and get at least 11 feet in the broad jump. His shuttle times should stand out.

24 Malik Willis
Liberty, quarterback

Willis, who in person looks like a muscled-up linebacker, has one of the most powerful arms the draft has seen in a long time. At 6-foot, 225 pounds, Willis has tremendous wheels with great elusiveness to complement his speed, having run a 4.50 40. His burst is evidenced by a 38.5-inch vertical.

25 Quay Walker
Georgia, linebacker

Walker is about 6-foot-4 and 245 pounds and has an 80-plus-inch wingspan. He flies laterally and has speed to close. He should run in the 4.5 range. Scouts are still a little split on how instinctive he is, but he sure gets there in a hurry.

26 George Karlaftis
Purdue, edge rusher

The biggest recruit the Boilermakers have landed in a long time lived up to lofty expectations and should prove to be a very good, productive NFL player, based on his excellent athleticism and relentless work ethic. The 6-foot-4, 275-pounder played on the U-16 Greek national water polo team as a 13-year-old and later became a two-time Indiana state champion in the shot put. He also started for three seasons on his high school basketball team. He's run a sub-4.70 40 in college and vertical jumped 37 inches. He's also broad-jumped 10-1.

27 Dominique Robinson
Miami-Ohio, edge rusher

The former high school quarterback spent three seasons playing wide receiver in the MAC before moving to the defensive line, where he blossomed with his 82 1/2-inch wingspan and terrific change of direction. The 6-foot-4 Robinson expects to weigh close to 260 pounds and run the 40 in the 4.65 range. At Miami, he ran a very impressive 4.31 agility time and also has vertical jumped 34 inches.

28 Matt Henningsen
Wisconsin, defensive lineman

Henningsen was a Campbell Trophy semifinalist as one of the top scholar-athletes in college football. Don't sleep on the 6-foot-3, 293-pound former walk-on's athleticism. At Wisconsin, he hit 19.34 mph on the GPS. In pre-draft training, he has clocked a laser-timed 1.59 10-yard split and has also vertical jumped in the mid 30 inches. He might crack 10 feet in the broad jump.

George Karlaftis - No. 26

29 Armani Rogers
Ohio, wide receiver/tight end

He's a wild card in the draft process and an interesting prospect. He played quarterback at UNLV and Ohio and showed his speed last year by setting an NCAA record for quarterbacks with a 99-yard touchdown run vs. Buffalo. Word is, at 6-foot-5 and 230 pounds, Rogers has been turning heads now that he's training as a receiver due to his size and speed. He's vertical jumping in the high 30s. He has run the 40 in the low 4.4s and has been broad jumping around 11-feet. It's probably a stretch to think that, even if he wows scouts at his pro day, a team drafts him, but he'll likely earn a shot in someone's camp.

30 Chris Olave
Ohio State, wide receiver

He's torn up the Big Ten over the past three years, catching 33 touchdowns. Simply put, the 6-foot-1, 190-pounder is effortlessly fast. It probably wouldn't shock anyone if he clocked a 4.30 40.

31 Dareke Young
Lenoir-Rhyne, wide receiver

The next Freak from Kyle Dugger's Division II alma mater is very raw. The 6-foot-2, 220-pound Young's jumping numbers will stand out, though. In training, he's vertical jumped 40 inches and done 11-2 in the broad jump. He has a 40 time of 4.45 to go with 20 reps on the bench.

32 Tycen Anderson
Toledo, safety

One of the best-kept secrets in the MAC, Anderson has excellent ball skills and range. At 6-foot-2, 204 pounds, he's expected to run the 40 in the 4.4s and also should vertical jump around 40 inches.

33 Brandon Smith
Penn State, linebacker

The Nittany Lions have had more than their share of Freaks — and while the 6-foot-3, 240-pound former five-star recruit isn't Micah Parsons as a player (who is?), he's still very, very explosive. He's expected to run the 40 in the 4.4s. He has broad jumped in 10-5 and vertical jumped 36 inches. He also timed 4.25 in the shuttle last offseason.

34 Zander Horvath
Purdue, running back

The No. 40 has produced a lot of standouts at Purdue, and Horvath follows in that tradition, having led the team with 746 all-purpose yards. Horvath is intriguing. He's 6-foot-1 1/2, 232 pounds and runs the 40 in the 4.4s. He's clocked a 2.53 20-yard split, timed 4.06 in the short shuttle and also bench pressed 225 pounds more than 30 times.

35 Nakobe Dean
Georgia, linebacker

The electrical engineering major is brilliant off the field and on. He was the leader of the Bulldogs defense. He doesn't have great size — maybe 5-11 1/2, 225 pounds — but he's a blur on the field. Rival coaches think he'll run the 40 in the 4.4s and should have really quick shuttle times.

36 David Ojabo
Michigan, edge rusher

The Nigeria native was emerging fast in Ann Arbor opposite Hutchinson. Ojabo is expected to run the 40 in the low 4.5s and vertical jump in the high 30s.

37 Michael Griffin Jr.
South Dakota State, safety

A big physical safety at 6-foot, 215 pounds, Griffin's on the list for his explosiveness. At South Dakota State, he vertical jumped 42 1/2 inches and broad jumped 11-1. He also clocked a 4.47 40.

38

Lucas Krull
Pittsburgh, tight end

The one-time San Francisco Giants draftee reportedly used to clock 98 mph on the mound. He has grown into a 6-foot-6, 255-pound NFL prospect and emerged as a nice weapon for the Panthers last season, catching 38 passes for 451 yards and six touchdowns. Pitt coaches think that, despite his big frame, he can still run the 40 in the 4.6s.

Lucas Krull • No. 38

39 Zion Johnson
Boston College, offensive lineman

An All-ACC lineman, the 6-3, 310-pound Johnson had an impressive week at the Senior Bowl, showing off the good athleticism and intelligence that makes him a versatile option. Johnson, who has vertical jumped 34.5 inches at BC and completed 32 reps on the bench, is a very underrated athlete. He's also a single-digit handicapper who played high school golf despite his big frame.

40 DaMarcus Mitchell
Purdue, edge rusher

He transferred to Purdue from junior college and flashed some potential, but his athleticism will get him some long looks. The 6-3, 260-pounder, who has only seven percent body fat, runs the 40 in the 4.6s, has broad jumped 10-5 and vertical jumps in the high 30s.

Just missed the cut

Trent McDuffie, Washington, CB; DeAngelo Malone, Western Kentucky, edge rusher; Treylon Burks, Arkansas, WR; Nik Bonitto, Oklahoma, edge rusher; Logan Hall, Houston, DL; Damone Clark, LSU, LB; Isaiah Weston, Northern Iowa, WR; Calvin Austin, Memphis, WR; Otito Ogbonnia, UCLA, DT; Carson Wells, Colorado, OLB; Dameon Pierce, Florida, RB; ZeVeyon Furcron, Southern Illinois, OG; Chase Lucas, ASU, CB; Will Adams, Virginia State, CB; Jequez Ezzard, Sam Houston, WR; Malcolm Rodriguez, Oklahoma State, LB; EJ Perry, Brown, QB; Dallis Flowers, Pittsburg State, CB

Calendar of Events

Jan. 17: Deadline for underclassmen to declare for NFL Draft

Jan. 28–29: HBCU Combine

Jan. 29: NFLPA Collegiate Bowl

Feb. 3: East-West Shrine Bowl

Feb. 5: Senior Bowl

Feb. 19: HBCU Legacy Bowl

March 1–7: NFL Scouting Combine

March–April: On-campus pro days

April 28: NFL Draft first round

April 29: NFL Draft second and third rounds

April 30: NFL Draft fourth through seventh rounds

May 6–9 or May 13–16: Rookie minicamps